"The most memorable travel writing, from Marco Polo on Kubla Khan's concubines, to Bruce Chatwin on aborigines, is about a different kind of journey, one that takes the reader on an exploration of the jungles of the soul. Mary Morris's account of her travels is very much in the tradition of these interior voyages."
—*Chicago Tribune*

"Compelling... *Nothing to Declare* is impeccably, internally timed."
—*The New York Times Book Review*

"Remarkable...always completely honest... Morris's book is positively inspiring."
—*New York Woman*

"Morris paints a deft and devastating portrait of bored, side-tracked American expatriates, passing year after year in the bars and restaurants of San Miguel, chiefly in the company of each other."
—*Mademoiselle*

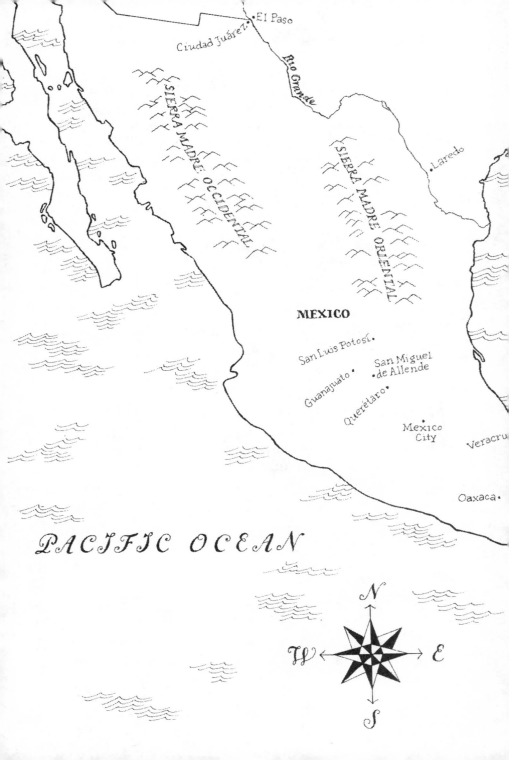

UNITED STATES

$\mathcal{GULF\ OF\ MEXICO}$

CUBA

Puerto Juárez
•Mérida
Yucatán
Peninsula
•Isla Mujeres

$\mathcal{CARIBBEAN\ SEA}$

San Cristóbal
de las Casas
•Palenque
Tikal•
Flores•
BELIZE
San Pedro Sula
•Roatán
Tuxtla
Gutiérrez
Zinacantán
GUATEMALA
La Ceiba
Jocotán•
Chichicastenango
HONDURAS
•La Entrada
Copán
Tegucigalpa
Tapachula
Quezaltenango
Lake Atitlán
Panajachel
Guatemala City
EL SALVADOR
NICARAGUA
Managua•
Masaya
Lake
Nicaragua
COSTA
RICA
PANAMA

Also by Mary Morris

Fiction
Vanishing Animals and Other Stories
Crossroads
The Waiting Room
The Night Sky
House Arrest
The Lifeguard

Nonfiction
Wall to Wall: From Beijing to Berlin by Rail
Maiden Voyages: Writings of Women Travelers (ed)
Angels & Aliens: A Journey West

MARY MORRIS

NOTHING
TO
DECLARE

MEMOIRS OF A WOMAN
TRAVELING ALONE

PICADOR USA   NEW YORK

To Guadalupe Martinez Medina and the Children of San Antonio

Picador® is a U.S. registered trademark and is used by St. Martin's Press under license from Pan Books Limited.

For information on Picador USA Reading Group Guides, as well as ordering, please contact the Trade Marketing department at St. Martin's Press.
Phone: 1-800-221-7945 extension 488
Fax: 212-677-7456
E-mail: trademarketing@stmartins.com

All the names in this book have been changed except for those of Lupe and her children, to whom this book is dedicated.

ISBN 0-312-19941-4

First published in the United States by Houghton Mifflin Company

First Picador USA Paperback Edition: January 1999

10 9 8 7 6 5 4 3 2 1

1

THE DESERT

THERE ARE ONLY TWO WAYS TO GET TO SAN Miguel. One is to drive north from Mexico City. The other is to drive south from Laredo. There is also a train but I only saw it once in the time I lived there, and it was two hours late. The road north from Mexico City is unremarkable — a superhighway to Laredo, lined with Pemex stations, auto part shops, tire retailers. It is also lined with many foreign factories, such as John Deere Tractors, Singer, Volkswagen, Pepsi, companies that find prices right and labor cheap south of the border.

If you are driving north from Mexico City, after about four hours you reach a turn. If you miss the turn, you can go straight back to America in about ten hours flat. But if you leave that main road and turn left, toward the west in the direction of San Miguel, as I did one summer in what seems now like a long time ago, you enter a different world. The kind of world you might read about in the works of Latin American writers such as Fuentes, Rulfo, García Márquez. Macondo could be out there.

You come to the old Mexico, a lawless land. It is a landscape that could be ruled by bandits or serve as a backdrop for the classic Westerns, where all you expect the Mexicans to say is *"hombre"* and *"amigo"* and *"sí, señor."* It is a land with colors. Desert colors. Sand and sienna, red clay and cactus green, scattered yellow flowers. The sky runs all the ranges of purple and scarlet and orange. You can see dust storms or rain moving toward you. Rainbows are frequent. The solitude is dramatic.

You come abruptly to the high desert, where people travel on the backs of burros and everything slows down. Cactuses are huge and resemble men in agony, twisted and wild; it is a trail of crucifixions.

I have a friend named Brenda Reynolds who was living in Mexico City, and it was Brenda who drove me to San Miguel the first time. She was preparing to move back to the States just as I was arriving, but she offered to take me to San Miguel, spend a night, and help me get my bearings. Brenda was one of the people who suggested San Miguel when I told her I wanted to live away from the United States for a while. Brenda said it was a perfect place and that the weather was wonderful. I had heard other things about San Miguel as well. Americans who want to get away often go there. It is a place of exile.

I had grown weary of life in New York and had some money from a grant, so I felt ready for a change. With a terrible feeling of isolation and a growing belief that America had become a foreign land, I headed south. I went in search of a place where the land and the people and the time in which they lived were somehow connected — where life would begin to make sense to me again.

When I arrived in Mexico City, Brenda served me black zapotes. A black zapote is a fruit somewhat like a giant prune which, when mashed with sugar and lemon juice, with the skin and seeds removed (an incredibly arduous task), tastes like something they'd serve in heaven. There is no comparable way to describe this dish except to say that it was the first thing I tasted when I arrived at Brenda's house in Mexico and I thought then that I had come to paradise.

This was before driving to San Miguel, before I traveled down that very dusty road with Brenda, laughing the whole way until we approached San Miguel. Then I grew serious, struck by the reality of the place to which I had come. As we twisted on those hairpin turns, a street sign appeared. It contained the silhouette of a full-bodied woman and beneath her the words *curva peligrosa* — dangerous curve.

. . .

I never saw pictures of San Miguel before I moved there, but I went with a very clear sense of what everything should look like, a cross between New York and my hometown and the island of Crete — exciting, familiar, and foreign all at the same time.

The Buddhists are right in their belief that expectation is one of the great sources of suffering. We try to direct the scripts in our heads and are miserable when we fail. We often wonder why things go better — parties, journeys, love — when we have no expectations. What I saw as we drove into San Miguel bore little relation to what I'd thought I'd find. A dusty town rose out of a hill, with a salmon-pink church spire and pale stucco buildings. Buses were everywhere, idling near the center of town, sending up exhaust that would make me choke whenever I walked past. Their drivers shouted the names of destinations unknown to me — Celaya, Guanajuato, Dolores. Tortilla ladies and avocado ladies sold sandwiches near the buses as blind beggars and naked children, broken-spirited donkeys and starving dogs, filled the streets.

I was missing the fine points. Expectation does that to you. I missed the bougainvillea, the colonial buildings, the cobblestone streets. It is easy to miss all of that once the panic sets in. I only saw the dust and the donkeys and the strangers and a place that seemed so distant from anything I thought I could ever call home.

That night Brenda and I checked into a hotel where I drifted into despair. I had no idea how I was going to live in this place. I couldn't believe that I'd packed myself up and moved to a strange country where I barely spoke the language and didn't know a soul. My purpose seemed vague, and walking those streets for the first time, I told myself that I should just get back in the car and go home. We had dinner and strolled, hardly speaking. I was quiet, withdrawn, and Brenda, who has always respected my privacy, did not pry. Perhaps she suspected that something had happened to me before I left, but she did not ask and I didn't say.

In the morning we went to a hot spring nearby called Taboada, a place I would frequent on Sundays because the hotel there served a wonderful brunch. The Mexicans frolicked with their families, often fat, happy, splashing out of control, and I longed to be that carefree again. Afterward we drove back to the hotel and Brenda was ready to go. Like a scoutmaster sending a boy out on a survival training course, she left me with a Spanish-English dictionary, a few extra pens, and the name of the woman who ran the Blue Door Bakery, who supposedly had rooms to rent.

I was on my own. I had no idea what to do with myself. It grew dark early and I wasn't ready for bed. Instead I went out for a walk. The streets were dark and cobbled and smelled of garbage. I didn't know my way as I wandered through the back alleys and narrow roads. I passed restaurants with crowded tables and lighted rooms where families stared into the blue light of miniature TVs. Old women, grasping babies, sat telling stories and laughing on doorsteps. I searched for a movie house, a coffee shop with guitar music, but all I found were dozens of bars filled with men, and I wasn't ready to go into one alone.

I walked to the center of town, to a square lined with benches and trees, which in most parts of Mexico is called the zócalo, but in San Miguel is called the jardín, where an odd procession passed in front of me. A circle of girls walked in the clockwise direction around the perimeters of the jardín, perhaps half the distance of a square city block. There were at least a hundred of them. And encircling them, moving counterclockwise, was a group of young men. Hesitating, I cut through their circle and sat down on a bench, where I watched as the single men and women of the town encircled each other on and on into the darkness in this ritualized form of courtship — called the promenade — which would occur every night at the hour when the birds came home to rest in the trees of the jardín.

They flirted and giggled and pretended to ignore one

another, but as darkness fell, some wandered off, boy leading girl away to a more secluded spot in a darkened street, an alleyway. I imagined them whispering each other's names and thought of how far I was from someone who might whisper mine.

The church bells rang. From the steeple clock that seemed to rule over this town and mark the monotony of the days, I saw that it was only nine o'clock. I still had much of the evening ahead of me and no place to go. Then I noticed the people entering church. Toothless old men and corpulent women with babies wrapped in shawls shuffled in. Girls in miniskirts with white blouses held the hands of boys in green or cranberry polyester pants; others in blue jeans, black hair slicked back, lingered in the alcoves.

In this town of shrieking birds and promenading lovers, I could think of nothing else to do, so I went to church. I walked hesitantly into the large Gothic stone building and down an aisle toward the apse. Slipping into a pew off to the side, I sat beside a campesino family, the woman with a child suckling at her exposed breast, the children in freshly ironed shirts, the father, in a sombrero, keeping a toddler from running away.

I sat down with a blind man and with wide-eyed children, with the toothless, the ancients, the impoverished, the illegitimate mothers, the crippled, the drunk, the miserable, the lost. I prayed with the beggar who had no hands and with the woman whose eyes were empty sockets. I prayed with the contrite and the forlorn, with *los desdichados* — the unlucky, the misfortunate. I prayed until the tears came down my face and I was crying in that church on that Sunday night, my first night alone in Mexico, praying that the reason for this journey would be made clear to me, oblivious of the Mexicans who watched with troubled eyes, moved by my inexplicable grief.

THE WOMAN WHO RAN THE BLUE DOOR BAKERY did have rooms to rent and at dusk the next day she took me to see them. We drove down the hill away from the center of town. We left the cobbled streets with bougainvillea vines and turned up a dirt road lined with mud huts, garbage, diseased animals, children in tattered rags. When I asked where we were going, she replied, "San Antonio." And that was all.

She was a cold, calculating person whom I would simply call "the Señora" and who'd take only cash for rent. In the middle of these slums in the neighborhood called San Antonio, the Señora had built some town houses. One of them hâd been vacated recently, and she showed it to me. It had a living room, kitchen, and small patio on the ground floor. Two bedrooms upstairs. Upstairs the front of the town house had French doors and a small balcony, but the back wall had no windows. I should have suspected that someone was building a house on the other side, but I did not. The sound of construction would punctuate my days. A small, winding staircase went to the roof, where I'd read and do the wash in the afternoons. From the roof I could see the sierra — the pale lavender hills and the stretch of high desert, the cactus men and wildflowers.

It was the only place I considered. "I'll take it," I said.

I never would have moved to the neighborhood called San Antonio if I'd known better. For that part of town was different from the other parts. Very few Americans lived there. It was too far from the center of things. I would have to walk half an hour up a dusty hill to get to market. It was the poorest part; it was where the servants who served the wealthy lived and where others struggled just to get by. It was the dustiest, dirtiest place, where the Mexicans would call me *"gringita"* and my own mother, when she heard me describe it, would beg me to leave. I had no idea what I was doing when I moved into San Antonio. But I am grateful for the mistake I made.

I had come to Mexico with two suitcases and an electric typewriter, and the next day I brought them by taxi to my town house, whose name I noticed as I dragged my belongings from the cab: the *Departamentos Toros* (bull apartments). I am a Taurus and as I stood beneath the sign with the name of the apartment, I thought this must be a good omen, to move into a place named after my astrological sign. I spent the day settling in. But as dusk came, I realized I knew no one, was about a mile from town, and had no food in the house.

Climbing the winding stairs to the roof terrace, I saw the vast Mexican desert stretching before me, the sun setting in strips of brilliant scarlet across the horizon. The town with the pink steeple of the church seemed far away. I saw the birds — large, black, noisy birds — which every evening at dusk flew to the center of the town to stand guard over the promenade. And then, as I'd do many evenings after that, struck by the prospect of the evening alone, I followed them.

I changed my clothes, put on a pair of walking shoes, and headed up the hill — a climb I'd never get used to. But I went to the place where the birds were going. It seems I have always followed the birds, or have wanted to follow them. The loud chirps, thousands of them, grew piercing as I approached the jardín.

The birds were bedding down for the night and the promenade was in process. I sat on a bench to watch. It is odd to sit in a place where you know absolutely no one. There was not a familiar face, not even the possibility of someone passing whom I might know. I was here a perfect stranger.

After a while I got up and headed down a road. I paused in

front of a bar lit in amber. Inside Mexican men drank and laughed. There were no Mexican women, but there were a few Americans, so I thought it would be all right. I went in and ordered a beer. I sat for perhaps half an hour, until it grew dark. People were all around me and I thought to myself how I should try to make conversation, but I found I could think of nothing to say. I was sure that someone would come up to me and say something like, "Been in town long?" or "So where'd you come from?" But no one did. I ordered another beer and nursed it slowly, realizing I did not want to go home. I watched the people around me. Mexicans laughing and talking with blond American women. Other Americans huddled in corners. One man, whom I'd later know as Harold, sat in his pajamas, which he wore when he went on a binge.

I took it all in, and then, at about ten o'clock, I walked home. I descended the hill, toward the bus stop, until I reached the turnoff to San Antonio. At the turnoff is the dirt road, about a quarter mile long; it is walled on both sides. If you are attacked while walking down this road, you have no place to go.

For the first time, I walked that quarter mile at night alone. Every shadow, every sound, made me turn. I behaved like a hunted thing. It is not easy to move through the world alone, and it is never easy for a woman. You must keep your wits about you. You mustn't get yourself into dark places you can't get out of. Keep money you can get to, an exit behind you, and some language at your fingertips. You should know how to strike a proud pose, curse like a sailor, kick like a mule, and scream out your brother's name, though he may be three thousand miles away. And you mustn't be a fool.

Brace yourself for tremendous emptiness and great surprise. Anything can happen. The bad things that have occurred in my travels — and in my life in general — have happened because I wasn't prepared. At times I wonder that I am still alive.

A GIANT WHITE ROOSTER STOOD ON MY SMALL balcony at five in the morning, greeting the dawn. He was so loud it seemed as if he were in bed with me. I opened my glass doors and tried to shoo him, but the rooster wouldn't leave. That was when I noticed the yard on the other side of the wall, perhaps only a dozen feet away, where my neighbor lived.

In Mexico, there are many walls whose purpose is to keep poor people away from rich people. Often the tops of these walls are decorated with bits of broken bottles — Coke, Pepsi, Seven-Up — to deter people from climbing over them. There was the wall that lined the road to San Antonio. And between my house and the rest of Mexico was a wall eight feet high.

From my balcony I looked into the yard and saw lumber, debris, mud, a pig, a lamb, animal droppings, chicks, assorted articles of clothing, and no vegetation. A radio played mariachi music over the sound of running water and scrubbing. Somewhere beneath a makeshift wood-plank shelter a woman was doing the wash under a small light.

I put on my robe and went outside. The sky was a deep shade of blue-green and the rooster continued its dialogue with the other roosters of San Antonio. I climbed on a large stone by the wall and pulled myself up as far as I could, shouting. A few moments later a woman peered down at me. I could barely make out her dark face in the blue-green light of morning, but she had thick black hair and weathered skin, a brilliant smile. "Excuse me," I said in my broken one-year-of-college Spanish, "but is that your rooster on my balcony?"

She looked up and shook her head. "He is always on the

prowl. He hates to stay home," she said in dismay. "Like all men."

The next thing I knew she had come around to my side of the wall and we went into my apartment. She seemed to know the place well. Without a word, she went upstairs into the bedroom and onto the balcony, grabbed the rooster by his legs, and carried him, flapping, out of the house.

I tried to go back to sleep, but the feathers floating around my head and the sound of the radio and the woman's comment about the rooster and men stuck in my mind. Finally I fell asleep until about ten o'clock, when I heard someone knocking.

I opened the door and found two small children. "My mother," one of them whispered, holding out a napkin, "asked me to give you these." I could barely hear her as she handed me the napkin. I opened it and found five corn tortillas, still hot. "What are your names?" I asked them. They said nothing. "Where do you live?" They pointed to the other side of the wall. Then they ran away.

That afternoon I climbed the hill to the market to go shopping for the first time. The market was about a mile's hike from San Antonio — a long, steep climb that takes about half an hour. Then suddenly I was bombarded by the market.

Honeycombs covered with dead bees were thrust into my face. Huge chunks of brown mescal that look like caramel, red and black zapotes, papayas and mangoes cut open for sampling, cactus ears, cheese, garlic, long-stemmed gladiolas, juice stands, polyester dresses, pottery, watermelon. I paused at the herbalist who sells his bark and wood chips, dried grasses and flowers, roots and herbal teas, to cure your insomnia, kidney failure, weight loss, tension, headache, infertility. I was struck by it all, from the flowers to the stench of the butcher's unrefrigerated meats. There was beauty and filth everywhere as wasps buzzed the candy man and sucked the exposed sugar, and diseased children, selling corn, flicked maggots from their eyes.

I bought chicken, rice, avocados, beans, wild honey, and mangoes, which was more than I could carry. After a few blocks, I had to stop at the jardín to rest. I had not been there long when a man sat down beside me. He was a handsome Mexican with a camera around his neck. "So how long've you been in town?" he asked in good English. I told him I was new. He introduced himself. "Guillermo Gonzalez," he said. He was a photographer and offered to help me with my bags. He carried them down the hill as far as the turnoff to San Antonio. And then he said, "Why don't I pick you up tonight and take you to La Fragua."

"La Fragua?"

"Yes, it is the place where most people go. I'll pick you up at six and introduce you to some people I know."

I made myself an early dinner and got dressed up. At six he had not shown, so I read. I read until seven, then seven-thirty. When he still had not shown, I decided to go into town on my own. I was not yet accustomed to Mexican time, nor to being stood up. I put on lipstick and headed out the door.

I was ready to climb the hill when the rains broke. They came out of nowhere and I rushed back inside. Within moments torrents had fallen on my enclosed patio. My windows were a sheet of rain. I went up to the roof and from the small shelter where I would do the wash, I watched it come down. Gray rain swept across the high desert, a rain that would bring incredible wildflowers and turn the hills into an easel of color with cornflowers, primrose, buttercups, and lavender thistle, but I didn't know this at the time. I went downstairs as dusk fell and the rain continued and I sat reading, waiting for the rain to cease. But it did not. It kept coming. It came longer than any rain should have come. And then, just as the night began, the electricity failed. The lights went, leaving me in darkness.

I was caught completely unprepared. I had no light to read by, no candles, no batteries for my flashlight. I had no television or radio or phone. No one to talk to, no one to see, no plans for seeing anyone, no way back to the life I had known.

I listened to the endless buzzing of mosquitoes as they bit me. I listened to my own breath. I told myself that in a few hours it would be morning. All I had to do was sleep. Instead I listened to the whisper of two lovers who sought refuge beneath the awning of my porch. I was perhaps no more than five feet away from them. They did not know I was there as they panted and caressed and made sounds like animals into the night.

I woke to the sound of sweeping and the bleating of a lamb, so I stumbled downstairs and opened the door. There I saw a woman with a distended belly and strong, crablike arms and legs. Her skin was dark and her thick hair was tied up in a loose bun. She wore a miniskirt, to which a small child clung. It took me a moment to recognize her as the woman who lived on the other side of the wall.

I wished them good morning. The children hid their faces and giggled. The one ducked beneath the lamb, hiding her face in its fleece. The woman brushed the strands of hair off her face. We introduced ourselves. Her name was Lupe and she said she took care of the property of the Señora who ran the Blue Door Bakery. Her youngest daughters were Lisa, who was four, and Cristina, who was two, nicknamed Pollo because she was scrawny like a chicken. The lamb was Pancha.

I was not sure what to say in this first conversation, so I asked Lupe if she knew where I could buy plants for my house. "Flowers?" she asked. And I said yes, flowers. I told her I wanted flowers. Living things.

Lupe said she would take me if I'd wait while she changed her clothes. I had wanted to work that morning, but since she was offering, I felt I could not say no. I asked her if it was far and she said no, *"No muy lejos."* Not very far. She dragged Pollo off with her and left me with Lisa and the lamb.

I asked Lisa, "Is that your lamb?"

And Lisa said, "Yes."

"Is he your friend?"

And she said, "Yes, he's my friend."

"What will you do when he gets big?"

And she said, "We're going to eat him."

In a few moments Lupe returned in a clean dress, her hair combed neatly, pushing a wheelbarrow into which she plunked Pollo. She grabbed Lisa by the hand and told me to follow. Thus Lupe, Pollo, Lisa, me, and the doomed lamb, Pancha, set off with wheelbarrow in search of the elusive flower lady.

We climbed up a hill over cobblestones, across the open sewer that would bring typhoid and dysentery and in some instances death to those who drank from it. In the heat and dry sun of the morning we climbed, farther and farther, into the poorest section of San Miguel, deeper into San Antonio, past mud-and-plank shacks where hungry children sat and scrawny dogs with open sores begged until I thought I could stand it no longer, and after about half an hour I asked, "Is it much farther?" and Lupe responded, "No muy lejos."

While I sweated and ached just from moving up and down hills, Lupe pushed and laughed and trudged. I have no idea where she took me or how long we walked, but eventually we reached a dusty road and there, along the side of the road, sat a one-eyed old woman in a shawl, selling flowers and plants at a good price. I picked a half dozen or so and felt suddenly embarrassed as I pulled money out of my wallet. The plants cost less than ten dollars, but I was slowly realizing that ten dollars would feed all Lupe's children (she had six at the time) for a week.

But I bought the flowers because that was what we'd come for, and we surrounded Pollo in bougainvillea and some house plants and a rose bush. Then Lupe proceeded to push the wheelbarrow back to where we'd come from. When I offered to help, she laughed. She said I was weak and she was strong. She made a muscle and made me feel it. She told me she was old but strong. I asked her how old and she said thirty-six. I told her I was thirty-two. She laughed and said I was old, too.

LUPE BEGAN TO COME TO MY HOUSE OFTEN AND we'd sit in the kitchen and talk. She told me the story of her life in inconsistent bits and pieces. I strained to understand. My Spanish, which had been a requirement in college, was a necessity now. While I was often mute, like some aphasiac who comprehends but cannot speak, I grasped much of what Lupe said. And as time went on, without my paying much attention to the process, we would carry on real conversations. But for now I mostly listened to what she said.

At different times she gave me contradictory information. Sometimes she said her parents were ranchers who died in a fire, leaving her with a cruel grandmother. Other times she said that her father left her mother bereft and her mother died of grief. But the story Lupe told most often when she came to sit and drink coffee was the story of how her father had been a landowner from a rich gentry of high birth, and her mother, a poor Indian. She said she knew this story only through what was whispered to her at markets or, as she walked the dirt roads of San Antonio, from the rumblings of *brujas* — witches — in the hills, all of which composed the little mosaic that made up her past.

Lupe first told me this after we had not known each other long. It was a dark night, but with a large moon, and we sat in my darkened living room. She said her father had taken her mother on a night not unlike the one we were talking in, because her mother was so beautiful with her long black hair, silken, which hung to her waist, braided. I pictured this woman, dressed in sackcloth but exquisitely beautiful in the moonlight, her hair glistening, her body trembling and afraid.

Lupe did not know the details, but I often wondered how it had happened. Had the *patrón* called for her and she had to go to him? Or did he go to her hovel, where she lived with her aging father and brothers? Her father, I imagine, knew what the patrón wanted when he came and knew there was no choice but to let her go. He could not fight after so many years tending the patrón's fields, planting his seeds, watching his crops. But her brothers, what about them? Did they expect a better position from the patrón because he had taken their sister? Was this part of the deal?

I believe the patrón went to Lupe's mother's shack and took her somewhere into the fields as was his custom because he could not take her back to his house where his indolent and portly wife and children slept. He took her to the spot where he'd taken all the other women, a smooth bank by a stream where a willow dipped into the waters, and there he undressed her. He admired her skin, olive and soft in the moonlight. He caressed her silken hair. She could not have been more than eighteen. When he touched her, she shivered and pulled away.

But soon she began to wait for him. Perhaps because he was skilled, even gifted with women, she learned to like it, and even to anticipate his visits. She would go to the well and wash her hair and her skin. She would look at her reflection and begin to think about what it was that made the patrón desire her.

And then, when she was with his child, the patrón withdrew. He pretended he did not know her. Perhaps he sent some money to the family, some baskets of food, perhaps he put one of the brothers in charge of the corn crop for a season, but that was all. He did not come again. Now her days stretched themselves into a solid line of abandonment and grief. She had grown to depend on his caresses. Her belly grew. Her brothers said nothing. Her father said nothing. No one spoke of it. No one acted as if anything had happened at all.

Then one night she went out to the fields when the moon

was high, and she went to the spot by the stream where the willows dipped their branches into the water. And there she lay to give birth. She clutched her wrist in her mouth, or thrust a branch between her teeth, and gave silent, writhing, solitary birth.

What did this woman feel as the child slipped from between her legs, a wet, bloody mess, a lonely child born to a lonely woman? I like to think she thought about the child first. About what was best for her.

She nursed the child once. Then she carried it to the door of an old woman and left it there. Afterward she disappeared. Perhaps she let herself be carried away by the shallow water of the stream. But I think she wandered into the sierra, where she remained hidden in the hills. She was an invisible woman and it was easy for her to escape. A woman without substance, the one no one saw.

2

IN THE SIERRA

IT WAS MY MOTHER WHO MADE A TRAVELER OUT OF me, not so much because of the places where she went as because of her yearning to go. She used to buy globes and maps and plan dream journeys she'd never take while her "real life" was ensconced in the PTA, the Girl Scouts, suburban lawn parties and barbecues. She had many reasons — and sometimes, I think, excuses — for not going anywhere, but her main reason was that my father would not go.

Once, when I was a child, my parents were invited to a Suppressed Desire Ball. You were to come in a costume that depicted your secret wish, your heart's desire, that which you'd always yearned to do or be. My mother went into a kind of trance, then came home one day with blue taffeta, white fishnet gauze, travel posters and brochures, and began to construct the most remarkable costume I've ever seen.

She spent weeks on it. I would go down to the workroom, where she sewed, and she'd say to me, "Where should I put the Taj Mahal? Where should the pyramids go?" On and on, into the night, she pasted and sewed and cursed my father, who it seemed would have no costume at all (though in the end my bald father would win first prize with a toupee his barber lent him).

But it is my mother I remember. The night of the ball, she descended the stairs. On her head sat a tiny, silver rotating globe. Her skirts were the oceans, her body the land, and interlaced between all the layers of taffeta and fishnet were Paris, Tokyo, Istanbul, Tashkent. Instead of seeing the world, my mother became it.

I have always had an excellent sense of direction and my mother always trusted it. Looking back now, I think she was crazy to do so. When I was fourteen, she decided she had to see Europe, so she got me a passport and let me wander freely through the great capitals — London, Paris, and Rome. Once, as our taxicab sped through London streets, we saw a fruit vendor selling peaches and my mother said, "God, I'd love some peaches." When we got to the hotel, she went to rest, and I made my way back through the streets.

I returned two hours later with a bag of beautiful peaches. Since then my mother has never concerned herself about my wanderings. She has never pictured me lost. I have never felt her afraid.

I never told either of my parents the truth about the places I'd been. My father would write me newsy letters, photocopy them, and send copies to every American Express office in Europe or China or Central America, hoping I'd show up for my mail. And I'd write back chatty notes about going to the beach or visiting a native market. I never told them about the earthquakes in Mexico, the near-rape in Jerusalem, the searches of Soviet border guards, the mud slides in Bolivia. They have come to assume that somehow I'll return, safe. So far, I have.

How do you know if you are a traveler? What are the telltale signs? As with most compulsions, such as being a gambler, a kleptomaniac, or a writer, the obvious proof is that you can't stop. If you are hooked, you are hooked. One sure sign of travelers is their relationship to maps. I cannot say how much of my life I have spent looking at maps, but there is no map I won't stare at and study. I love to measure each detail with my thumb, to see how far I have come, how far I've yet to go. I love maps the way stamp collectors love stamps. Not for their usefulness, but rather for the sheer beauty of the object itself. I love to look at a map, even if it is a map of Mars, and figure out where I am going and how I am going to get there, what route I will take. I imagine what adventures might await me even though I know that the journey is never what we plan for; it's what happens between the lines.

I have never really been disoriented except when I come out of the New York City subway and can't figure out whether I am facing east or west, uptown or downtown. But otherwise I have always instinctively found my way and in this I feel blessed, as if somehow I am intended to be a journeywoman, a wanderer of the planet, and, I suppose, of the heart.

I have been, and am, a woman who has often found herself, through circumstance and fate, alone. Nothing terrible has ever happened to me. I have had close calls, but I have never been raped or wounded or kidnapped or tortured. But I have been left and betrayed, bewildered and afraid.

Sometimes it is difficult, but I try to read other maps. Maps of my own inner landscape, of dreams and of the outcome of the events of my life, of the warnings and signs of others. When I see danger, I step away. When I think I can move forward, I move ahead, and when I think I can come closer, I do. Sometimes I am wrong, but often, if I pay attention, I am right, and these maps of my own instincts guide me as surely as any by Rand McNally would.

I come from the Midwest, from the bluffs along the shores of Lake Michigan. It is not an exotic place, though it is very beautiful. You might stumble on an arrowhead, and there are a few trees, bent and tied to the ground a century before by Indians, which mark trails. But other than that, there is nothing remarkable about the part of the world I come from. Nothing extraordinary ever happened to me in the years that I was growing up, except once.

One day as I was coming home from school, I spotted a bird, larger than myself, sitting in the lower branches of a tree in a wooded area I passed through every day. It was huge and peered down with dark, curious eyes. It appeared weary and a bit confused, surprised to find itself in a tree in the Chicago suburbs, yet it stretched its wings and fluttered them with tremendous dignity. I spent the better part of an afternoon watching until my mother, half crazed, came searching and found me entranced by a bald eagle.

The eagle, off course from its home in the wilderness, had somehow landed in my neighborhood. Though lost, it seemed sure of itself. I wondered then as I wonder now what led it to suburbia, so far away from where its nest should be. At times I have thought it just wanted to get away, to go somewhere else. I knew it would find its way.

It was the first traveler I ever encountered and it made me thirsty to take a trip. Whenever I find myself somewhere I don't think I belong, I remember the confidence of that lost wanderer. I have tried to imitate it.

SAN MIGUEL DE ALLENDE IS NOT A DANGEROUS place, not a threatening place. It is true that there is no doctor you can trust to give you a shot. It is true that if you are in an accident or have a heart attack, you are probably a goner. That there are few phones or televisions or viable communications with the outside world. But it is not a place of upheaval, beset with soldiers, disease, or crime. Yet it does have its share of poverty, which most Americans who come here do not see.

I have been to dangerous places and San Miguel is not one of them. I have seen men plucked off buses in Guatemala and carted off by soldiers. In hospitals in Nicaragua I have seen boys with half their stomachs blown away. I've spent an evening with terrorists in the old city of Jerusalem and been in blackouts orchestrated by Shining Path in Lima. In Manhattan I have had a knife put to my throat while a trembling boy said he was going to kill me for my bicycle.

These are the average dangers that happen to those who move through the world. But San Miguel de Allende is not like those other places. It is a beautiful town which has been declared a historical monument by the government of Mexico in order to preserve its colonial style. Set in the high reaches of the Mexican desert, it has perfect weather, perpetual spring; the so-called winter consists of a bit more rain and colder nights. The days are always warm and dry, the shade cool. There is no humidity. Mexico City is five hours away by bus. There is no reason to go there and be afraid.

And yet I can say that I have never been more afraid in my life than I was in San Miguel. Camus has written, "For what gives value to travel is fear. It breaks down a kind of inner structure we have. One can no longer cheat — hide behind the hours spent at the office or at the plant (those hours we protest so loudly, which protect us so well from the pain of being alone)." I was afraid in part because of what my neighbor, Trevor Helstrum, told me, but mostly I was afraid because of what I carried in my heart.

San Miguel was founded in 1542. The name Allende was added later, to commemorate the hero of the independence, Ignacio Allende, who was born here. Facing the broad sweep of the Laja River and the distant blue of the Guanajuato Mountains, the town sits at six thousand feet above sea level, on a steep hillside.

Most of the sixty thousand inhabitants of San Miguel are Mexicans — campesinos, workers, shopkeepers, children (there seem to be millions of children). The Mexicans work in the fields, on ranches and haciendas. They work in construction or in the small shops in town. Most are extremely poor.

But perhaps a thousand of the inhabitants are Americans. Expatriates can live well, a mere ten hours from Laredo if you drive fast and don't break down in the desert heat. There are writers and painters, or so they call themselves. There are the former school teachers and moderately successful real estate brokers who come to live out their retirement days. There are the alcoholics, the Vietnam veterans, sixties burnouts, gay divorcees, people with a little pension.

There are the losers. Seth, the soldier who lost his leg in Vietnam, who said he was the only person in the history of the United States Army to refuse the Congressional Medal of Honor. (Later, when I did some checking, I learned he had never received the Congressional Medal, let alone refused it.) Irene, who had ten children and had left them all; she said she'd never been happier in her life.

Clifford Irving has a house in San Miguel. He went to live there after the scam of his Howard Hughes book. There was the gorgeous fashion model (we knew she was gorgeous because of the pictures of her all over her apartment) who had become a vegetarian fast-foot junkie, living on avocados and doughnuts. The wealthy widow from Manhattan carrying on a "serious" relationship with a campesino. Melanie, who had been having a long love affair with a prominent Catholic priest who had a political career; he had paid her way to San Miguel to keep her quiet. And Sam, the bitter black man who laughed when I sat on his toilet and came out screaming, my pants full of giant roaches.

Here were the mediocre Americans, the would-bes, the has-beens, the might-have-beens, with their meager pensions. The dollar is always strong and the peso always weak. There is no border with greater economic discrepancy in the world than the border between the U.S. and Mexico. First World meets Third World. The discovery of oil in 1978, the projected rise of the petropeso, did not help. Americans can always do well in Mexico. Life is cheap. For a hundred dollars a month we could live like kings in castles, away from it all.

Many times at the bus station in Querétaro, where I often had to change for the bus to San Miguel and where I could get a good, quick lunch of avocado and coriander salad and tortillas, I just sat and looked at the destinations on the buses headed north. The names of border towns — Laredo, El Paso, Nogales, Tiajuana — made me think how close I was to home. In truth I couldn't have been farther away. Sometimes I thought I'd hop on a bus and stare out the window, and in a day or so, I'd be there. But I never did.

I HAD BEEN IN SAN ANTONIO ABOUT A WEEK BEFORE I laid eyes on Trevor Helstrum, and when I did I found there was something about him that I disliked immediately; that feeling would only grow. There were four town houses where I lived, and Trevor, photographer, lived in the second one. One day he opened his door and introduced himself. He was a powerful man — tall with enormous hands and cruel, empty blue eyes. He wanted to know where I was going and when I told him to market, he asked me to pick up some vegetables for him. "If you bring me these vegetables," he said, "I'll have you over for dinner."

Trevor came from Pecos in West Texas. When we sat down that night to dinner of rice and beans and a shredded beef stew with green olives, he said, "The only thing I like about Mexico is that it's got a lot of fireflies, like Texas." I was going to comment that I hadn't noticed any fireflies, but Trevor went on. "I hate this place. I hate the flies. I hate the corruption, the poverty, the sickness, the way of life, the stupid Mexicans."

I cannot say I was enjoying myself much with this conversation, but the stew was good. "So," I said, "why bother staying?"

He ran his hand through his thick copper curls. "Why? Because it's cheap. That's why. No other reason. Cheap place for an artist to live." Trevor never struck me as being much of an artist and I don't remember a single piece of his artwork that I ever saw, but for whatever reason, he stayed in a place he said he hated.

After a few minutes Trevor took me under his wing. "Listen," he said, "you need to know the ropes. First" — he began before we'd finished our stew — "don't forget to check your bed at night and your shoes in the morning for scorpions. I woke up with one hooked to my backside the other night. It crawled right into bed and stung the hell out of me. There's two kinds. The black kind and the white kind. Mostly they got the black kind. They don't do nothing more than sting, but they also got the white kind and they'll work their poison slow into you and pretty soon you won't be moving so good, if you know what I mean."

"I get the picture," I said.

"I don't know why you moved into San Antonio," he continued. "The Mexicans, you know, they're pigs and you've moved into the poorest section. Over there, beyond the wall, that's the rich section." He pointed toward the wall that ran along the road to San Antonio. "Here it's the poor and it's all pigs. There's a hole in the wall by the rich section. Have you found the hole yet?" I told him I hadn't. "Well, it's a big short cut. You can come through it at night, but they're gonna block it up soon."

"They are?"

"The rich people hate the people from San Antonio. Like I said, we're living with pigs. If I were you, a woman alone like this, I'd move to another part of town. The police, they don't care what happens to you. They don't care what happens to the gringas. There was a woman, Sarah, who was murdered, got her throat slit, just taking a stroll in the sierra." He pointed toward the hills near the edge of town. "Don't ever go up there by yourself. And I've got a friend named Cory. Some Mexicans tied her to a bed and raped her for three or four days. She says she lost count." Trevor opened another bottle of wine and poured me an eight-ounce glass. "Don't ever trust a Mexican. They'll rob you blind. They'll rape you. They'll toss you into a drainage sewer without a thought. Just be careful."

As I was leaving, he gave me his final piece of advice. "And get yourself into some kind of a routine or else you'll go crazy."

When I got home, I turned on all the lights and ran through the house, making sure no thieves or rapists were hidden in closets or underneath beds. I locked all the windows and the door to the roof terrace. I barred the front door with a chair. Then I checked every inch of my bed for scorpions. I'm not sure when or how I fell asleep, but I woke at four in the morning with terrible stomach pains and my Swiss army knife open at my side. My body was covered with dozens of welts and I was scratching at my arms. The room was filled with mosquitoes which I smashed frantically, my own blood popping out of them as they were crushed with a magazine into the wall.

By the time the mosquitoes were dead and the pains had subsided, the white rooster next door was crowing. I looked at the clock; it was five-thirty. I went up to the roof terrace. In the east the sky was a glazed turquoise; the moon was full in the west. Lupe had turned on her radio and I heard the scrubbing sound of her washing clothes. In the distance, on a neighbor's clotheslines, I saw white loons, brilliant like newly washed sheets in the moonlight.

I decided to follow one piece of Trevor's advice and begin a routine. I'd write in the mornings. In the afternoons I'd go for walks, take pictures, do watercolors, write letters, and meet with the friends I was going to make.

I went to my typewriter that morning for the first time. Sitting down at my desk, I flicked on the switch. Nothing happened. I flicked it on again. Still nothing. I thought perhaps something was wrong with the electricity in my apartment, so I went next door to Lupe's to ask.

I had not yet been to her house. Lupe had a small wooden door with a string through it for a latch. I knocked and at first there was no answer. I knocked again and the door opened. A large man, bare chested, with strong arms and a muscular torso, stood in front of me. He had dark, deep-set eyes and a square jaw. He was very handsome and seemed to know it. From behind him three or four children played, some of whom I recognized. Others I'd never seen. He stepped back and motioned for me to enter.

I walked into a narrow cement vestibule filled with sheep droppings, bits of tortilla. He pulled aside a curtained doorway and I walked into one of Lupe's two rooms. It was a large, airless, cement-and-brick room with one tiny window. The room was dark and the air heavy with the smell of bodies and mildew. But it was tidy and clean.

The man, who I'd later learn was the father of Lupe's younger children, introduced himself as José Luis and sat down. He said that Lupe was not home. I told him there was no electricity and he laughed. "There never is," he told me, "after it rains."

"Oh, and how often is that?"

"Oh, every day for the next two or three months." I groaned, thinking of my electric typewriter and the work I'd planned to do, but he just shrugged. "This is the season. The lights go off all the time."

It had taken my eyes some time to adjust to the room around me, but now I could see the walls. They were covered with pictures of naked women — women with giant breasts, women with their asses in the air, women coyly hiding their pubic hair. Wanda, the Sex Goddess, her gold hair covering her nipples, stared at me. Margarita, the Nympho, and Isabel, the Nurse, revealed all. The Wonders of Feminine Beauty were on display — mostly from pin-up magazines, and they were tattered.

José Luis had papered the room where he and Lupe slept with these pictures. Now he looked at me oddly. In the dim, smelly room, surrounded by naked women, his deep breathing filled the dark.

A few hours later the lights came on and I sat at my desk to work. I flicked on the typewriter and was happy to be working until I noticed the stucco walls around me, which were black and seemed to be moving. The molding of the window I faced was black and crawling. I ran screaming from the house, calling for Lupe to come and help me.

That was when I met Jerry, knocking on Trevor's door. "Please," I said, breathless, "it's grotesque. It's horrible."

"Now, baby," he said, "just stay cool." He had a weathered face and a graying beard. He wore a T-shirt with a big rainbow on it, and a peace sign around his neck.

"Please, can you help me?"

Jerry, a writer from Maine, had gotten an NEA grant about ten years before and had been living in Mexico since then, trying to finish his novel. "It's a cross between Kerouac and Henry James," he told me in my apartment, as he swatted the walls with a rag. "With a little Dos Passos thrown in."

"Can I read it?" I said, not knowing what else to say to that description.

"Sure, when I'm done." I had a sense that that wouldn't be very soon. He told me he'd spent five years working on this one. He'd spent ten years before that writing another novel about impotence which nobody wanted to buy. "They all said it fell flat," he said, laughing.

I laughed, too, not because it was funny, but because it was ridiculous and because I had not laughed in a week. I watched as Jerry swatted flying ants. Soon carcasses lay all over my floor. After the ants were killed, he sat down to talk. I made him coffee and eggs. I thought about my promise to make a routine for myself. I would begin tomorrow.

Jerry was smart and would have been smarter if he hadn't smoked marijuana every afternoon in order to "get started." He was thrilled to meet "a real writer." When I invited him for dinner that night, he said, "Groovy." He said he'd bring Trevor and Trevor's girlfriend, Eleanore.

Lupe came by in the early afternoon. Her *compañero*, José Luis, said I'd been looking for her. I told her about the electricity and the ants. She nodded as if she knew all of this. "The ants come out of the cracks in the walls," she said, pointing. "It's the rain. I'll get you some spray."

"Why don't we go to market together?" I asked her. "I've invited people for dinner."

Lupe ran off and came back wearing a cotton minidress, black sandals, her hair combed and pulled up. She had Pollo and Lisa on her arm. I found the hole in the wall where Trevor had described it to me and we took the short cut through the rich people's neighborhood. Then as we trudged up the hill, I told Lupe I had met José Luis that morning. "He is a very handsome man," I told her.

"The worst kind," she said with a laugh. "All the women want him."

I said I'd seen the pictures of naked women in their bedroom. "Doesn't that bother you?" I asked. "You don't mind?"

She smiled. "There are worse things to bother me," she said. "They are his artists. He keeps them because they are artists."

"Is he your husband?"

Lupe shrugged. "He is the man I am with now. I had a husband, but he left for El Paso ten years ago with another woman. I haven't seen him since. He is the father of my three oldest children." I had seen three grown women near the house and these, she told me, were her older daughters. "I've been with José Luis a few years. These other children are his. Except for Agustín. He has another father."

"Oh," I said, wondering if I felt judgmental. I decided I did not.

"I had some birth control but it fell out. I don't know what it was. I told the doctor I didn't want more children and he gave me something, but it never worked." She paused and looked at me. "Do you have a husband or children?"

"No," I said, "but I'd like both."

"It is very difficult for men and women to get along," Lupe said. She tugged on Pollo and Lisa, dragging them along with her. "It is all very difficult. José Luis gives me fifty pesos a day to feed my children. It is not enough. I barely make do. That is why I work for the Señora of the Blue Door Bakery. Still, it is not enough. But I keep the apartments nice for her and she gives me a little money and the house to live in."

Lupe helped me pick out a good chicken and nice avocados. She said she would help me make my dinner. We walked down the hill in silence, and when she saw I was having difficulty with my parcels, she took them from me. When we got to the house, she said, "I'll make José Luis something to eat. He cannot eat unless I feed him. If I did not feed him, he would die. It is better," she said, "not to depend on anyone."

I WAS READY FOR DINNER AT SEVEN, BUT NOBODY showed up until eight-thirty. The first to arrive was Jerry, who apologized for being on Mexican time. He said, "How ya doing, baby? Had any more plagues?" He kissed me on the lips.

I made him a drink and he raised his glass. "To peace and happiness. To staying cool."

Trevor and Eleanore arrived at nine, also apologizing. "You know, no phone. No way to let you know."

Eleanore was blond and studying painting at an art school in town. She brought me a small statue of a donkey and Trevor brought me a bottle of tequila with a worm in it. I thanked them for the gifts.

I had made chicken, rice, beans, and a salad. I had scrupulously washed each leaf of lettuce in halazone, but Eleanore wouldn't touch the salad. Jerry kept putting his hands on me and finally I asked him not to. He said, "You're so uptight, baby. This is Mexico. Cool out," and he raised his glass. "Peace, happiness."

He put his arm around me again and I said, "I can't eat with your arm around me."

Then Jerry announced, "I'm a good judge of people and Mary is a real New Yorker."

"I come from Illinois," I said.

"Well," he said smugly, "you're sure different from the down-home folks here."

I said, "I just don't like to be touched by people I don't know."

And he said, "Look, I'm simple, I'm not complicated. I just put my arms on you to comfort you. You need comforting."

He was going to drive me nuts. "If I need comforting," I said, "I'll ask for it."

[35]

"You know what," Eleanore said, "apropos of nothing, I come from Medicine Hat, Canada. Do you know the entire population of Medicine Hat is equal to the population of Mississippi?" I stared at her blankly.

Trevor turned to me. "Isn't that incredible?"

I was bored so I offered to read their palms, something I can do, though I don't like to waste or abuse my powers. I saw that Jerry was going nowhere fast and probably didn't have long to live, but I told him he would publish one of his manuscripts, which he did. Eleanore would leave Mexico soon and I told her that. Trevor was a mean, dangerous person, someone to stay away from, but he would be successful in his career, and I told him that.

Then I began to grow serious and I told them other things. I told Jerry he had been married briefly years before and his wife had been untrue. He had never told this to anyone and he had never fully recovered. I told Eleanore her parents' divorce had broken her heart. I told Trevor he had a teen-age son with whom he was out of touch and that this had bothered him lately. As I spoke, the flame in the fireplace dwindled and we finished off the wine. I couldn't believe my accuracy. They sat back, amazed.

La Fragua is the Ritz Bar of San Miguel. The next evening I met Trevor, Eleanore, and Jerry there. They introduced me to Cory, the woman who had been raped by the Mexicans. It is a rather nice bar in an open courtyard, where musicians tinker at the piano and alcoholic Americans show up in various states of disintegration.

Trevor was telling some horrible story about his friend T.C., a black guy living in San Miguel, who had gotten branded, literally branded with a branding iron, on his arm in a fight after a soccer game. Jerry was furious because I hadn't spent the night with him, and wouldn't talk with me. Then Eleanore and Trevor suddenly began having a fight. Eleanore kept saying, "So go back to Texas, I don't care." And he kept saying, "All you care about is the way you look." I wondered why I was seeing these people again, but loneliness makes you do strange things.

Cory was a quiet blond girl with a dour look. So, I thought to myself, this is what a woman who has been tied to a bed and raped looks like. When I got up to go to the bathroom, Cory followed me. As we were combing our hair in front of the mirror, she said, "So who gave you the shiner?"

My hand went instinctively to my face. I hadn't thought it could still be seen. "Oh, it's almost gone," she said, "but I'm sort of an expert in that kind of thing."

I looked in the mirror and saw a darkened line beneath my left eye. "I got it at a softball game," giving my usual line.

"Mexican or American?"

"American," I said with a laugh.

Cory said, "They're all the same. I guess you've heard the rumor about me being raped."

I stopped combing my hair.

"I wasn't raped," she said. "I'd been dating this Mexican cab driver." She was unbuttoning her blouse. "Look what he did to me." She undid her blouse and displayed her breasts. Her nipples were completely swollen; her breasts were black and blue all the way to the armpits. "He twisted them," she said. "He twisted them till they turned black and blue." Then she said softly, "I thought you'd like to see what we have in common."

I didn't want to think I had anything in common with Cory. I had been dating someone that spring and he hit me once. We had been having a stupid argument, over nothing really, and the next thing I knew he had struck me with his closed fist. No one had ever laid a hand on me before, but I had been with men who were violent with words. I had been with men who were cruel to me. But after this man struck me, something changed. I felt my life turn upon a different course.

Cory was buttoning her blouse, looking embarrassed now. "I don't know why I did that," she said. In a matter of days she would leave for the States, and I never saw her again. "I guess I wanted to show you," she said, "that you aren't alone."

SAN ANTONIO REACHES BACK TOWARD THE SIERRA, sloping upward from my house, and the next day I climbed farther into the district of San Antonio than I had ever climbed. I had never gone that way before, but on this day I decided to go. At first the children from my neighborhood followed as I climbed to the place where people lived not in houses but in adobe-like shacks, made of wood slats and clay, with no water or electricity. The children called out my name as they tagged along, but after a while, they began to turn back.

I climbed to where the smell was terrible and I was surrounded by filth, droppings of all kinds — chicken, pig, goat, cow, human. I was struck by the stench of rotting meat, left out with no refrigeration, covered with maggots, the stink of rotting vegetables, of garbage, of all kinds of refuse, but I kept climbing.

Children I'd never seen came alongside of me. These children were dirty, with snot on their faces and matted hair, and they pulled at my arms and legs. They followed me to the open sewer that separated San Miguel from the sierra. The open sewer was unbearable, and as I jumped across I was afraid that I would fall in. But the only way into the hills is to leap across it and so I leaped.

I headed across the sierra where Trevor had told me not to go, where he said the murder of Sarah had taken place. I wasn't sure why I was going there, but I told myself it was to pick wildflowers. In truth I had no intention of picking flowers. Something drew me to these arid hills and I knew I had to go. I tried to keep the tales from Trevor out of my mind as I climbed higher and higher into the sierra in the heat of the day, away from town.

As I walked I passed Mexicans herding sheep, carrying dried twigs back from the hills. I saw boys kicking soccer balls and women walking with jars of water on their heads. But soon I was on a trail that followed the edge of the sierra, and there were no more people. I could hardly see the town as I climbed. I thought about Sarah having her throat sliced, and at first I was frightened.

Then I saw the hummingbird. It was a green humming-bird, translucent, vibrant, its color that of emeralds as it hung, suspended in midflight, over the heart of a yellow cactus flower in the sun.

I know something about hummingbirds. Their hearts beat a thousand beats per minute. They are so frail that if you hold one in your hand, it will die of fright. Theirs is one of the most delicate beauties in nature. Yet they have enormous strength. Try flying backwards or dangling in midair. It is more difficult than forward motion. I was once told that hummingbirds expend more energy for their weight than any other living creature, that if harnessed they could solve the world's energy problems.

But to harness that beauty is to destroy it. I stood perfectly still — my own heart beating — calm and unafraid in front of a force of nature, a gemlike green bird, suspended before me, fragile yet strong.

Then it occurred to me that I was being watched. I don't know how I knew this, but I felt eyes upon me. I didn't know from where. It was just a sense that someone was out there, watching me. I climbed farther and then I stopped.

At the mouth of a cave about a hundred yards away, an old woman stood. She wore a white shawl over her head, but I could see that her hair was jet black, even though her face was wizened and she appeared incredibly old. I waved and she extended her arms toward me, not in a welcoming gesture, really, but almost in benediction.

I moved toward her, but she raised her palms and motioned for me to stop. I did not come closer, but I stared. I could not help feeling that I had seen her somewhere before, that I knew her, though I was sure it could not have been in this place or even in this time. I turned for an instant to look at the trail behind me, and when I looked back toward her, she was gone.

IN MY APARTMENT IN NEW YORK I SURROUND myself with familiar things. Pictures of my family, mementos from friends, angels I collect to guard over me. There is a picture of my grandmother's family, her ten brothers and sisters, my great-grandmother and great-grandfather, shortly after their arrival from Russia. They are in front of a backdrop, a bucolic setting of a picket fence, rosebushes, a cloudy summer sky — a setting none of them would ever know. They pose turn-of-the-century style, hands on each other's shoulders, sister to brother, mother to father. These are people who belong to one another.

My great-grandmother looks rigid, severe. She will die an early death. My great-grandfather is different. There is something sensual in his lips, a warmth to his eyes. I would marry him if I could. But the children seem to take after the mother. No one is smiling. It does not look as if they have much fun. Many of them are twins. Buni and Dave. Herman and Hezi, each with a single blond curl, thick as an ice cream cone, rolling down his forehead, who opened a lumber yard together at the end of the First World War. My grandmother, Lena, whose twin, Mary, died shortly after birth. Now as I write, Dave is ninety-nine and paralyzed with a stroke. All the others are dead. Eva, Morris, Hannah. My uncle Dave told me once that his first memory was this: In his town in the Ukraine, when he was six, he buried a dog alive in the mud. When he told me, he laughed out loud. I cannot imagine having a first memory like this.

My first memory is of my mother. We are living on Roscoe Street, which means I am less than two, and my mother says I cannot remember this, but I am sure I do. We are going somewhere. I am dressed in blue and my mother wears beige. She is yelling at me, telling me terrible things, and I am not crying. I am stubborn, standing still. When I tell this to my mother, she says I am a liar. She says I have made it up. Pure invention. I never raised my voice to you, she says.

In my apartment there are pictures of my mother, with her long red hair, riding a pony. Another picture of her, older, in a cowgirl outfit, waving a hat, looking incredibly slim and beautiful. And then later still, a woman with gardenias in her hair. And there is that picture of my father, cigarette in his mouth, in front of a Model T, still a gay bachelor, years before they met.

All of this is in my memory now. I have brought nothing with me. No pictures of friends, dead pets, old boyfriends, parents, nephews, siblings, the house I grew up in. It is all behind me. In memory and remembrance. I have brought nothing to recall my former life, none of the smells or textures or tastes or faces or roads or landscapes I have known before.

Sometimes at night I lie awake and try to remember a certain person's features. Or his scent. There was a man I loved. Not the one who hit me, but another. And I try to piece him together, like a jigsaw, but I cannot find his substance. I try to do the same with my family, but I feel orphaned, adrift. Sometimes I think there are ghosts in my room. I have felt, from time to time, my grandmother's presence. But even the ghosts are insubstantial as ghosts. My life has lost its résumé, its vita, its biographical note.

Like Lupe I exist here in the present. Lupe knows who she is only by what is whispered to her, what people have said. She does not know who she really is and what she will become. She makes up more stories for me. Her mother grows more beautiful, her father wealthier, with a ranch the size of Texas, her grandmother crueler by the day. I invent for her incredible loves I have known, a happy childhood, a brilliant career. But they are all the lies we use to prop ourselves up and I do not know why we need them.

.   .   .

I began to learn things from the Mexicans. The brujas, or witches, live in the sierra, and they can cast spells. Since some of the women of San Antonio had seen me climbing in the afternoons, they stopped to tell me things. They told me what to look for to find out if a curse had been placed on my head. My fruit would be full of worms. I wouldn't be able to light the fire. Plants would wither at my touch. They shared with me their fears. A howling dog was a dead man's song. If you fell down on a dark road, part of your body would go to hell.

I had not been living there long when a dead bird appeared, wings opened, nailed to a tree across from my house. One of the women stopped me on my way to market and pointed to the dead bird. She said that someone had put a curse on my house, but I had no idea who. I was told that a white witch was trying to counteract the bad spells, but I had to beware of the one who put the curse.

Early each morning noises woke me — running water, children playing, a bleating lamb. Every morning Lupe came to my house with one or more children. She handed me coffee and brought fresh flowers. One day I told her what the women said about the curses and she shook her head. "You are good in your heart," she said. "No curse is stronger than a good heart." In the morning I saw that the dead bird was gone and a red powder, like paprika, had been sprinkled on the tree. When I asked Lupe about it, she just smiled. "You are safe here," she said. "Trust me."

I went to Lupe for things I needed. For washing clothes I could not get clean, for cooking rice and making fideo soup — a soup with thin noodles. One afternoon when I wasn't feeling well, I left Lupe a note which I wrote in my then ungrammatical Spanish. It read, "If you are going to market, could you bring me some eggs, mangoes, and drinking water." I enclosed a hundred pesos. Later that day I found on my counter a plucked chicken, salad, and a six-pack of Dos Equis, plus change. When I saw Lupe next I thanked her for going to market for me and asked if she'd had difficulty with the note I'd left. She nodded and looked away as if she did not want to embarrass me.

Whenever I went to Lupe's, she slid her body through the door so I could not see inside. Once I said to her, "Lupe, I have already been inside. You don't have to hide anything from me."

She shook her head. "It is not for someone like you to see." But slowly she let me in.

I never went farther than I was invited. It took weeks to get past the first rooms she shared with José Luis and the three smallest children and the pictures of naked women. The three oldest children, the teenage girls, all of whom went to school every day, slept in a smaller room with a curtain for a door and one tiny window. One day when I ran out of cooking gas, I went next door to ask Lupe to help me find the gas man. The teenagers were home and they invited me in. They pulled back the curtain to their room and I sat down on their big bed. The room was infested with flies, but all their clothes were kept neatly washed and folded in trunks. Only a curtain separated them from the outside. I asked if that was enough and they rubbed their arms. "When it is cold," said María Elena, the oldest one, who was very tall and much too thin, "it can be terrible."

I knew Lupe for a long time before she invited me into her kitchen. It wasn't really a kitchen, though. The stove was a small pile of bricks where she burned coals. Pots and pans of rice and beans sat uncovered while flies hovered, and Lupe kept swishing them away with her hand. Buckets of water stood filled with dirty dishes. There was no icebox, no sink. "Where do you wash?" I asked, and Lupe took me out back. There would be no more secrets between us now.

In the yard I saw the wood-plank lean-to with a washbasin where water ran. Toward the back of the lean-to, near the wall that divided my house from hers, a slab of wood rested across a wooden seat; I knew this was their toilet. "Lupe," I asked, dismayed, "where do you bathe?"

She pointed to the washbasin. "In cold water?" She nodded and suddenly I saw she was ashamed. "The Señora says she will build us a bathroom when she is done constructing the apartments," she said, trying to save face, but she and I both knew that the Señora would never give Lupe a bathroom.

"You may bathe in my house whenever you wish," I told her.

She looked surprised. "There are too many of us."

"Whenever I go into town, all of you may bathe," I told her, and she understood that I meant this.

On Saturday night I went to the jardín, trying to decide if I wanted to go to La Fragua for a drink, when I saw Guillermo, the photographer who had stood me up when I first arrived in San Miguel. He saw me as well and came over. He sat down beside me. "I am sorry about our date," he said. "Something came up."

"Oh, it's all right," I told him.

"I am married," he said. "I have two children. I probably would have slept with you if I had picked you up, so I thought it was better if I didn't."

"What makes you think I'd sleep with you?" I asked indignantly.

"You are lonely," he said. "I can tell."

For some reason I started to cry. In fact I began to sob right there in the jardín, and Guillermo didn't know what to do with me. He let me cry and then offered to drive me home. But I preferred to walk. I walked down the hill and crossed through the neighborhood of the rich people. I cut through the hole in the wall and rushed into my apartment just as the rains came. It wasn't long before the lights went out and I had still forgotten to buy candles. I sat alone in the dark, drinking Kahlua.

Soon I heard laughter and voices, one of which was not unfamiliar. I pulled back the curtain and saw beneath the eaves Lupe's oldest, thin daughter, María Elena, soaking wet, in the arms of a boy I'd seen visiting her before. I wondered if they had been the lovers I'd heard when the lights went out for the first time. They must have seen me pulling back the curtain, because soon after I closed it, they were gone.

It wasn't long before there was a knock at my door. Lupe and the children stood holding candles. "You cannot spend another night in the dark," she said. I thanked her and they went away. Then I put the candles in a drawer to save for another night.

ON SUNDAY I DECIDED TO GO TO THE POOL AT THE Quinta Loreto, one of San Miguel's hotels. I took a book and my journal, but on the way out the door I ran into Trevor and Eleanore. They asked me where I was headed and when I said to the pool, they told me to wait; they'd come, too. I really wanted to go alone, but they seemed eager to join me. I knew only three Americans in San Miguel and I didn't feel ready to alienate these two yet.

When we got there, we plunked down our towels. Trevor called me a bookworm as he fondled whatever it was I was reading, and Eleanore started asking me if I liked the Alexandria Quartet, which she was just reading. I told her I'd read it in college. She said it reminded her of the life she was living here in Mexico. "You know," she said, "you could write the San Miguel Quartet, how about that?"

My eyes wandered to the pool, where I saw a swimmer I hadn't noticed before. It was a small pool, perhaps half the standard size, and a woman in a tank suit and goggles was swimming lengths. As the voices of Trevor and Eleanore droned on and on and in horrid Spanish accents they ordered papaya punches from obsequious waiters, I found myself transfixed by this swimmer. Length after length she swam and I began to count them. I counted well over one hundred and realized she was swimming a mile in that small pool. I marveled at her determination and strength, at the beauty and evenness of her strokes.

For about forty-five minutes this woman swam and then she pulled herself out of the pool. She wore a cranberry bathing suit that revealed her athletic build. She had the elegance of some large aquatic bird as she shook her head of auburn curls, splattering water. She walked toward her towel and I stood up. "Excuse me," I said, "but where did you buy those goggles?"

"Oh" — she turned to me — "I got them at home in Washington. Would you like to borrow them?" She said it so simply and openly that I did not refuse. I had not had goggles on in perhaps ten years, but I put them on and adjusted them to my eyes.

I got into the water and began to swim, at first in slow, choppy strokes, but soon my breathing deepened, I developed a rhythm, something I had not done in a long time. My breath, my arms, my body, moved in harmony, and for the first time in months I felt as if I had control over myself.

I did not swim long, but when I got out the woman was there. I thanked her for the goggles and told her we were having lunch soon. She agreed to join us.

Catherine Wilde was an art therapist from Seattle. She was getting her master's in social work and had come to San Miguel to learn Spanish so that she could work with Hispanics in the barrio. All through lunch with Eleanore, Trevor, and me, she kept looking at her watch. I noticed a nervousness, an impatience, as if she were not interested in us at all.

Trevor kept asking questions like, "What's it like working with crazy people?" He said that people could tell him their problems for fifty dollars an hour anytime. Eleanore said, "I once went to a shrink when some guy broke up with me but decided what I needed was just a new guy, so I went and bought clothes instead."

After lunch and a rest by the pool, Catherine began to gather her things. "Do you want to keep the goggles?" she said. "I've got another pair."

"Sure, I'd love to keep them. Are you leaving?"

She nodded. There was something fiercely independent about her. I both admired and was frightened by it. "I'll go with you," I said, unsure if that was what she wanted me to do.

We strolled back from the Quinta Loreto to the center of

town. I asked if she wanted to get a watermelon juice and she said she did, so we went to La Terraza, a small restaurant with a patio on the jardín; they served all kinds of juice drinks. "What're you doing with those two?" she asked.

I laughed, sipping my watermelon juice, which tasted very cold and sweet. "You mean Eleanore and Trevor. I've met only a few people so far."

She nodded. "Have you been here long?" I told her a few weeks. "I've only been here a few days," she said, "but I'd stay away from them."

She asked me questions about what I did. I said I was a writer. "A writer. Oh, that's interesting." It would be a full year later, in Seattle, as I handed her a copy of my first published book, that she told me she had never believed I was a writer because all the Americans in San Miguel said they were writers, but she'd liked me anyway.

She continued to glance at her watch, as if she had a pressing appointment. Finally I said, "Am I keeping you from something? Do you have to be somewhere?"

She laughed. It was, after all, three o'clock on a Sunday afternoon in San Miguel, Mexico, and it was highly unlikely that anyone had anything pressing to do. "No, it's just a bad habit. I always feel like I've got to be somewhere, even when I never do." She twisted her watch around her arm so that she could not see it without making a significant effort. "I'm sorry I do that." She softened. She had nervous lines in her face, but they faded as she relaxed. "You know, last night, when the lights went out? I had no candles, nothing. I sat in the dark getting drunk on Kahlua."

"Me, too." I laughed. "I've spent a lot of nights that way. Buy candles."

She said, "Yes, that's a good idea." She got up to leave. "Would you like to have dinner with me? Tomorrow night?"

I said I would. Just then we heard the sounds of a procession, so we got up to look. It was some sort of parade for the mothers of San Miguel, but it was all men dressed like women. They had melon breasts, enormous bellies, make-up. Some swept the streets or dusted park benches. Others cradled babies of rags. We watched in disbelief. Then Catherine said she wanted to get home.

We did not live far from each other and I walked her home. I said I would pick her up the next day at seven. Then I cut across the rich neighborhood to the hole in the wall. Slipping through, I noticed that bits of broken glass now appeared on the top of the wall — Coke and Fanta and Seven-Up — making it impossible to climb over. The glass shimmered and the shapes looked like animals and flowers against the dark.

That night my dreams were filled with men. Erotic dreams of men making love to me. Wild and impassioned, men I used to know, men I have never seen. My body trembled, orgasms of seismographic proportions ripped through my sleep. I did not know where they came from, but I felt that this was what it must be like to be brought back from the dead.

There was a man I loved named Daniel who had left me the year before. And he came into my dreams that night in San Miguel as he had come into my life the night before I moved to Mexico. That night — and this was not a dream, this happened, or at least I think it did — my doorbell rang at four in the morning. I put on a robe and walked downstairs. And there in the neon light of the vestibule I saw him.

He had been a student of mine and he was seven years younger than I. We had dated for two years and one day he just put the phone down and didn't pick it up again. That had been in June of the previous year. He was one of the reasons for my going to Mexico.

When I opened the door, I said to Daniel, "What are you doing here?"

He said, "I don't know. I don't know what I'm doing here." Then he looked at me. "Who gave you the black eye?"

I told him it was no one he knew. He stayed until dawn and we made love. Then, as the sun broke, he said, "I've got to get going."

I said to him, "Do you know that I'm moving to Mexico tomorrow?"

And he replied, "No, I didn't know that."

"Well, I am," I said.

"Well, then, I guess I came to say good-bye." And he was gone.

LUPE HAD A WAY SHE LOOKED WHEN SHE WANTED something. It was like a child. She couldn't meet my eyes; instead she stared at the ground and turned her foot. In the morning she came over to my apartment, dragging Pollo by the hand. "Could I ask you a favor?" I said she could. "Already," she said, "you have done me many favors."

"We are friends," I told her. "You have helped me here a great deal. They are not favors."

She said she needed a pair of shoes and so did Lisa and Pollo. She asked if I could loan her two hundred pesos, which at the time was about twelve dollars. She said it was an advance on work she would do for me and I told her it wasn't a problem to loan her two hundred pesos.

In the afternoon I saw Lupe in the street, shuffling through the dirt in the same broken sandals she had worn earlier that day. I called to her. "Where are your new shoes?" She glanced around to see if anyone else had heard and I realized I had embarrassed her. "They are inside," she shouted to me. She would show me later.

I stopped by for a visit. Sitting in her fly-infested kitchen, we made small talk. She gave me a recipe for "green chicken" and showed me how she made her beans so spicy. When the youngest children came up to me, I looked at their bare feet. "Where are your new shoes?" I asked. They looked ashamed and ran away. Lupe said she wanted to save the shoes for a special occasion. I understood somehow that she didn't want to show me the purchases she had made and I decided it was better not to pry.

I met Catherine at seven and we went to a little taco place for dinner. We both wore flowery skirts and peasant blouses, and we looked like sisters. I told her that I had seen a sign announcing an open house at the San Miguel branch of the American Legion. The American Legion was essentially a bar where soldiers hung out and played poker, but it was also where San Miguel's literary crowd went for beer and conversation. Catherine said she'd like to go. At dinner we talked in a more relaxed way. She told me about her boyfriend back home, named Tom, and I told her about Daniel and what a bad time I was having. She said, "You know, it's not easy to be a woman in our culture. I can tell you're smart. You're smart but you seem a little naive. You probably won't have an easy time."

"No," I laughed. "I can't say as I am having an easy time."

After our tacos, we wandered over to the American Legion. Some old soldiers were playing checkers. In a corner a serious poker game was in progress. Writers and artists were discussing their latest projects over glasses of cold Mexican beer. We were greeted at the door by a handsome Virginian named Derek Armstrong. He looked like a blond and compact Elvis Presley. "Well, howdy," he said. "You must be new in town. It's good to meet you. You don't look like soldiers, so you must be writers?"

"I used to paint," Catherine said. Then, pointing at me, "But she's a writer."

Derek ushered us to the bar and I noticed that he walked with a limp. He poured glasses of wine, sat us down at a table, and basically asked that we tell him everything about ourselves. "So, you've come down here to write?"

"Well, I came here to live."

"You can live cheap for a while."

I mentioned that I had a grant for my expenses and he seemed to move visibly nearer to me. His mouth opened and closed like a fish's. "You've got a grant. What kind of grant?"

I told him what kind of grant and that I had a book of short stories coming out and he moved closer still. Catherine winked at me and went to watch the poker game in progress. "Oh, so you're a writer. You know, I've been working on a

[53]

book — a novel about my experiences in Vietnam and about a man who is impotent because of the war."

I wondered why it was that every man in San Miguel was writing a novel about impotence. I felt it did not bode well for my social life. I wanted to retrieve Catherine but I saw that she had joined the all-male poker game. From the way she held her hand and leaned away from the table, she seemed to know what she was doing. Derek felt I needed to see the view from the rooftop of the building, so he took me upstairs, and on the roof he told me about a bisexual experience he'd had in the army; it made up the core of his novel.

"You see," he said, "my hero has a kind of infatuation with a man. I mean, they almost make love in a rice paddy, but then after the war, he's embarrassed by this and rejects his friend. Then he can't get it up with the wife he left behind." I really did not want to know all the details, especially the autobiographical ones, but he told me. And then he said, "Let's go back down. I want you to meet my girlfriend."

But before he had a chance to introduce us, Catherine joined me. She had actually won a few hands. "I always quit when I'm ahead," she said. "Listen, these people are creepy. I'm not sure I want to stay."

"Me either."

We decided to go to the bathroom, then depart. Together we went into the bathroom. When I saw it was not stalls, I started to back away, but it was clear that Catherine was not modest about such things. She hiked up her skirt and peed. She did not flush. "Your turn," she said. I hiked up my skirt and peed. Our urine mingled. I did flush. I was finally getting close to someone here.

When we went to open the door, it was jammed. We could not get out. We tried and tried, but it was impossible. At last we banged. Derek and some other people forced the door open and were surprised to find two women inside. "Sorry," we apologized feebly, and they all grinned at us, especially

Derek, who seemed to think he'd found some people he could really relate to.

Lupe began helping me around the house. In exchange I would bring bags of food whenever I went to market. Or, if she went to market for me, I'd give her extra money and say, "Buy yourself meat and we'll make a big stew this evening." Sometimes I'd leave her notes, which I now wrote in a careful and belabored Spanish, dictionary in hand, asking her to find the gas man or get some wood when the firewood donkey passed. But I'd ask for strawberries and find wild-flowers. Or I'd go for days without wood.

Finally one afternoon I asked her, "Lupe, are my notes poorly written?"

Lupe, who was washing dishes at the sink, did not look my way. "No, but I can't read them."

"Should I print instead?"

She kept running water over the dishes. "I can't read at all."

I watched her back, stunned. I had never met someone who could not read or write. I didn't know what to say. Finally I said, "Well, would you like to learn?"

"Yes, but I am too stupid and old."

"You are not that stupid," I told her, "and you are not that old."

I went into the other room and took out a yellow pad. On the top of the pad I wrote down her name. GUADALUPE, I wrote in big, bold letters. I recalled when I was a little girl and my father had done the same for me. We sat down together at the table. "This is your name," I told her, pronouncing it in an exaggerated way. "This is the letter *G*." I wrote the letter on a separate line. And for the rest of the afternoon Lupe sat at the table, struggling with the letter *G*.

I RAN INTO DEREK AT THE MARKET ONE DAY, AND he invited Catherine and me for drinks at his house. I left a note for Catherine at her guest house, something I did almost every day now, and said I'd pick her up. When we arrived at Derek's the party was already in swing. Mainly with Derek pontificating. He went on and on and in truth his stories were remarkable. "Let me tell you about my dog, Oscar," he said. "He was the most suicidal dog you'll ever meet. Used to love to dive off this four-story bridge and most of the times, except once, he lived . . ." He told us about getting arrested for shitting in Chapultepec Park. About being jailed in Mazatlán for trying to stop a bullfight. He told stories of cockfights and bullfights and about getting stopped by the *federales* between San Miguel and Santa Fe.

I met a guy named Arnold who'd written a guidebook to Mexico and he said he always got stopped by the federales. I looked at him, with his long hair and handlebar mustache, and thought how I'd probably stop him as well. They switched to mountain climbing and Derek tried to explain how it's all in the angle of your climb, and then he was back to the bullfights and assorted episodes of his obviously not so distant youth.

I was amused, but Catherine was restless and somewhat annoyed. She kept looking at her watch, rolling her eyes, making faces at me, indicating her desire to leave. But Derek was a terrific storyteller. I could not help but wonder if he could do on the page what he did over a few beers and shots of tequila with lime.

Then his girlfriend, Marnie, a mousy brown-haired woman with an ironic sense of humor, piped in. "Don't believe a word of this," she said to us. "He makes it all up. He says his stories come to him in his sleep — he gets up in the middle of the night, turns the light on, and writes it all down. He does his best work while he's asleep." She informed us that Derek slept under a mosquito netting, with ear plugs to shut out the noise and a retainer to keep him from grinding his teeth. She also told me in confidence that every day she locked him in his office and took the key, and he would write until four o'clock when she unlocked the door. I asked what would happen if there was a fire. "We just hope there isn't." She smiled.

I was thinking about leaving when the doorbell rang and two Mexicans walked in. One, named Carlos, was a friend of somebody or other and was definitely Spanish looking, with fair, European features. He came in, greeted us, and shook hands with everyone. His friend, dark-skinned with pure Aztec features, stood back in the shadows. Yet my eyes landed on him right away. He was tall, slender, and striking in an eggshell-blue shirt and jeans. He had a flat nose and high, sculpted cheekbones, deep-set dark eyes, and thick black hair. There was something about this man which struck me; it was as if a light emanated from him, a warm glow. He said his name was Alejandro. "But they call me 'El Negro,' " he said, the dark one.

They grabbed beers and sat down among us. They had driven up from Mexico City to visit Carlos's family in Guanajuato. Carlos was an acquaintance of Arnold, the man with the handlebar mustache. Alejandro sat near me and said he taught school in Mexico City. "What do you teach?" I asked.

"Metal crafts," he replied.

"That's the equivalent of shop," Derek put in.

"Alejandro makes beautiful things out of iron and brass," Carlos explained.

We didn't say much to each other that night but I told Alejandro where I lived. "Then I will come and have lunch with you tomorrow," he said. I was growing accustomed to

Latin ways and told myself I would believe this when I saw it. Catherine gave me a signal — a glance at her watch and a nod of her head — indicating she felt it was in my better interests to leave, and we set out for home. When we had dinner together in town, she usually walked me to the hole in the wall, even though it was out of her way. She took my hand and we walked.

When we reached the hole, we both paused, amazed. It had been cemented closed and the top of it was now completely covered with bits of glass, Coca-Cola and Pepsi bottles, Seven-Up, shards of U.S. soda pop bottles, to keep the poor people away. I'd have to go the long way around every night.

Catherine said she'd walk with me and we continued to walk hand in hand. When we got to my place, I asked her if she wanted to stay the night. We went upstairs and I gave her a nightshirt. As we lay in bed, Catherine told me things about her family and her past which she said she had not told anyone before. Her parents, she said, had both been alcoholics, and she had no recollection of them ever being sober during the first seven years of her life. When she was ten, her father, whom she adored, ran off and was never heard from again. She grew up in a house with her mother and brother and sisters and assorted half- and step-brothers from her mother's next marriage and thirty cats. "I'm a survivor," Catherine said. "That's all there is to it."

"How do you do it? What makes you so strong?"

She rolled over onto her back and stared at the ceiling. "I keep moving," she said.

"But what if you want to stop?"

She sighed. "So far, I haven't."

She looked at me. "You seem tense. I'll give you a back rub." I rolled onto my stomach and she raised my nightshirt. It was the first time I had been touched since I had arrived and the first time in a long time that I had felt good about being touched. I have no memory of falling asleep.

THE NEXT AFTERNOON ALEJANDRO DID COME OVER and stayed for *comida*. I was feeling poorly, coughing and with a headache, and he offered to cook — something he said he loved to do. He made a delicious chicken *molé* dish with an avocado salad and chicken soup. Though I was not very hungry, Alejandro insisted I eat. "You need your strength," he said in a motherly way.

We talked into the evening. We sat by candlelight and he spoke in a Spanish that was incredibly clear and precise, and I understood every word. His face seemed especially dark and carved in the candlelight, like the stone faces I'd visit among Indian ruins. He told me about his life and his family. He had a beautiful mother whom his father had divorced. He said that his mother always "did the streets," meaning that she went out and found men.

He had not seen his mother in many years. She lived in Mexico City with his two sisters, with whom Alejandro did talk from time to time. As he spoke of his mother, his eyes darkened and his mouth tensed. I felt there was something he was not telling, but that night I did not ask many personal things.

Instead he spoke of one of his nephews, who was blind. He said that the blind nephew knew things no one else could know. For instance, he'd say to his sister, "Uncle Alejandro will come today," though he had no way of knowing that on that day Alejandro would visit him at school.

Besides his nephew, he loved his father and brother. His father was a welder, a man whose trade was making wrought iron, and he'd taught Alejandro everything he knew. Alejandro was very good at fixing things and showed me how to fix radios and electric appliances. He said he could make elaborate gates and lawn furniture, but I never saw any of those. His brother, Ruben, was a musician. Alejandro seemed to worship these two men, but he seemed to have little respect for the women in his life; it seemed obvious that his mother had somehow broken his heart.

He stayed in my spare room and in the morning when I woke, sick with the flu, he had hot tea with honey and some kind of hot cereal waiting for me. He said that if I was up to it, that afternoon Carlos would take us to Atotonílco, a small, nearby village with a very old and sacred church.

I told him I'd like to go, but my head hurt and I felt a terrible pressure in my ears. "I have an old cure for you," he said. He lit a cigarette and told me to lie down. I asked him what he was going to do and he told me he was going to put the cigarette in my ear. "You aren't serious, are you?" I asked, but he said he was.

"This is what the witch doctors do," he told me. He inserted the filter end of the cigarette into my ear. From the corner of my eye, I could see little puffs of smoke coming from the cigarette that my ear was smoking. After a few moments, the ear popped and the pressure was relieved. He did the same thing to the other side. In an hour I was feeling better and ready to leave.

When we arrived at Atotonílco at around noon, pilgrims from all over Mexico were on their knees. Some, Alejandro said, had walked on their knees for miles, and their legs were bloody and raw. Many beat their breasts. Inside the church was a strange sight indeed. The very Indian-looking Mexicans in their tattered clothing, the men with sombreros pressed to their hearts, and the women with serapes wrapped around their heads, groveled and prayed, crawling up to a very white, Spanish, Goya-like Christ on the cross.

"You see," Alejandro said, "we pray to the white man's god. We have been conquered in this way. But behind the altar of this church," he whispered in a conspiratorial way, "where the Christ hangs, the men who built the church put their pagan, Indian gods. The gods of the Aztecs are hidden behind the cross. It is the secret of this church." Alejandro made the sign of the cross. "I have been taught to be a Christian," he said proudly, pointing to his Spanish friend, Carlos, "like him. But my heart is pure pagan."

We watched the pilgrims and afterward we walked to the house of a famous matador, Pepe Ortíz. His house, which was like a castle, had a beautiful waterfall. Then we walked into the *campos*, where we saw red birds, tanagers. Alejandro guided me by the arm as we walked. I could see that he was a gentle man with a good heart.

I had a friend once, an Indian mystic named Lalit, who told me that saints are not born, they are made. A person must work very hard to be good. As we walked the campos, a feeling came over me that came from deep inside. I could not pinpoint it, but I felt a great love within me. Not for a man or a woman, but for a way of being. A way of living I had not known before. The feeling seemed to come from this very place, from the ground we walked on.

That night I had a fever and Alejandro made me Aztec soup — a chicken broth with avocados and bits of fried tortilla. And again, as the night grew dark and the candles flickered, he did the talking. This time he told me about *el topo*, the mole. The story was a kind of parable, I think, about an animal that struggles in the darkness to get to the light, but when it reaches the light, it cannot see, because it has been living in darkness for so long. It has gone blind. "So, you see" — he folded his hand across mine — "you shouldn't look too long, or you may not even be able to see what it is you are looking for."

In the morning Lupe stopped by to ask me a favor. "May I ask you something?" she said, looking down and away. "It is Pollo's birthday on Saturday and I am giving her a party." She noticed Alejandro standing in the living room and she hesitated, then went on. "Would you bring your camera and take pictures?" I introduced Alejandro to Lupe and asked if

I could bring him with me. She said we would both be welcome.

On Saturday I loaded my camera. Alejandro and I went into town and bought Pollo a small dress, and at two o'clock I went to Lupe's. The place was swarming with children and animals and flies. The party was being held in the front room with the pictures of naked women. Lupe had decorated the room with streamers and everyone wore a hat. José Luis had a hat on. Even Pancha, the lamb, wore a hat. The pig kept running in and out as kids tried to put a hat on it. Chickens were everywhere Lupe served guacamole and a platter of fruit. There were at least twenty children and they all called José Luis "Papa," which I assumed was a term of endearment for an older person. It was only later that I learned they were all his children from various women.

Pollo wore a little blue dress. She was an ugly child with a wonderful smile and a great personality before the camera. Later a cake was produced. A gigantic pink cake with candles all over it. "Lupe, did you make this cake in my oven?" I asked, impressed and wondering when she had managed.

She smiled and shook her head. "You were out of gas. I made it here on my stove."

I had no idea how she had made a cake on an open fire, but she had.

I asked Lupe if today was really Pollo's birthday and Lupe said, "Oh, no, it was six months ago, but we are just celebrating it now." Lupe looked sheepishly at the ground and I looked down as well, my eyes following her gaze. She wore the same torn sandals she always wore and the children wore tattered shoes.

I understood that the twelve dollars she had borrowed had not been for shoes at all, but for this party for Pollo, and Lupe had been ashamed to ask me for money for the party. I don't know if she knew I knew, because we never mentioned it again.

On Sunday Alejandro and I, Catherine, and a man she had been seeing named Roger, who wore open Hawaiian shirts and walked around singing "The House of the Rising Sun," went for a hike in the hills near the Taboada hot springs, about ten miles from San Miguel. The countryside was much like that of the hills near San Antonio, but here it was flatter, which made it less windy but hotter, and more deserted. We climbed and climbed across the empty, dry sierra. I walked with Catherine for a while. "Are you serious about this Mexican man?" she asked me.

"I like him," I said. "And he is very kind."

Catherine seemed to reflect as we walked. "It wouldn't be bad for you to be with someone who is essentially kind."

We wandered the hills on a dusty plateau and suddenly, in the middle of that desert devoid of any houses or buildings, we came upon an Olympic-size swimming pool filled with sparkling turquoise water. At first no one said a word. We assumed it was a mirage. But then we reached it. I bent over, touched the water, and established that it was real. Alejandro did not like to swim and Roger didn't have a suit, but Catherine and I stripped down to our bathing suits, dove in, and began swimming laps.

There is an anecdote about Mexico which perhaps I should tell here. André Breton, founder of the surrealist school in France and writer of *Les Manifestes du Surréalisme*, was invited to Mexico in the 1930s to teach Mexicans about surrealism. He wanted a table so he hired a carpenter and asked him to build it. Breton drew an architectural drawing of a table, diamond-shaped, foreshortened front legs, long back legs; and the carpenter took the drawing and made a table just like the one in the drawing —diamond-shaped, with short front legs and long back legs. When Breton saw the table, he said, "I have nothing to teach these people about surrealism." And he returned to France.

The reality of Mexico is really a dual reality. On the one hand there is the original indigenous culture — mystical, magical, communal, given to sacrifice and the worship of pagan gods. And then there is the reality of the conqueror — logical, precise, efficient. These two cultures exist literally one on top of the other. They account for what seems the utterly contradictory character of the Mexican. As Octavio Paz has described them, Mexicans are eternal adolescents, unable to find their true identity and hence unable to grow up into the adulthood that identity brings.

Whoever built that beautiful swimming pool in the middle of a desert with no houses in sight I'm sure did it for what he thought was a very pragmatic reason, but it eluded us at the time. That swimming pool, perfect and clean, was for me what that table was for Breton. A glimpse into the Mexican character that defies the logic of the Western mind.

We had swum about ten laps when a campesino appeared. "Excuse me," he said, "but you cannot swim in this pool. My patrón does not allow it."

"And who is your patrón?" we asked. We looked at this man in his brown baggy pants and sombrero, standing in the middle of the Mexican desert with no road, no house, nothing nearby, this man who had suddenly appeared out of nowhere, out of the dust and the cactuses and the afternoon sun.

"He is a señor who owns this land and this swimming pool." His arm swept across a vast, empty expanse of land.

"But where is his house?"

"He has not built his house yet. He cannot afford the house. He has only built the pool."

We looked around. There was not a foundation, not even a marker for the house. And we had no idea where the campesino had come from. We tried to bribe him to let us swim a few more laps, but he was adamant and clearly afraid that he would get into trouble. Reluctantly, Catherine and I pulled ourselves out of the pool, and we left.

3

THE JUNGLE

ON THE PLANE TO TUXTLA GUTIÉRREZ, I SAT between a Cherokee Indian and a woman from California who was a nurse. The plane was a local, traveling via Veracruz and Minatitlán. We got into a conversation about pagan gods. The Cherokee told us that in Mexico many Indians still practice the ancient rites. He said that they act like Christians, but in their hearts they are all pagans. He himself worshiped the sun, the earth, and the stars; the sky was his church. The nurse asked if the stars were big or small. Incredulous, I said they were big. The Indian said they were there. They asked where I was going and I told them that I was meeting a friend in Chiapas. He told me to look for Lacandon Indians. "They practically live in the Stone Age," he said. "You'll know one if you see one."

We flew over parts of Mexico I'd never seen before. The lush tropical vegetation of the coastal regions was suddenly interrupted by giant smokestacks, oil refineries, and industrial development. The landscapes changed. At Veracruz the Indian and the nurse got off the plane. Then we left the gulf and flew inland. At Minatitlán the houses were on stilts, the roofs thatched. A black, smoky sky clouded the tropical beauty.

I was about to enter the land of the Maya. Current theory of human migration tells us that the indigenous peoples of the Americas originated somewhere in central Asia, that they crossed the Bering Strait and swept down through the North American Pacific Coast, spreading out east across the Rocky Mountains and the Great Plains, and moving south through the land that would become Mexico, through Central America, and finally into South America. The great civilizations of this migration in Central and South America were the Aztecs in Mexico; the Maya in the area of present-day southern states of Mexico, including the Yucatán and Chiapas, and Guatemala; and the Incas in the Andes of Bolivia and Peru.

Separated by distance, history, and eventually language, these peoples developed differently. However, the indigenous peoples of the region known as Mesoamerica — the area that covers the northern Mexican deserts to the lowlands of Honduras and El Salvador, the Caribbean Sea to the Pacific Ocean — shared many traits absent in most other places of the world. These include hieroglyphic writing, a complex calendar, specialized markets, a fairly homogeneous diet of maize, beans, and squash (which exists today), and a religion that featured self-sacrifice and mutilation as well as a pantheon of gods, including the rain god (Chac, to the Maya) and the renowned plumed serpent, Quetzalcóatl.

The great period of Mayan civilization, known as the classical period, was from A.D. 300 to 900. Its theocrats were generally believed to be a peaceful people who enjoyed science and the arts and who shunned warfare, unlike the Aztec rulers, who gained control of the valley of Mexico through conquest. The cities of the Maya, which traded with one another, formed a loose confederation.

In the tenth century the Mayan civilization was still at its peak. When its art and cities, its building and trade, were flourishing, it was abruptly ended by a mysterious event that no one has been able to determine. The Mayan hieroglyphics have never been completely deciphered. All we know is that a civilization that was at its height suddenly ceased.

The Maya of San Cristóbal came from a group called the Tzeltalans. They flourished in the central area of the Maya until about A.D. 400. Then they returned to the highlands, to the area around San Cristóbal. The descendants of the group — the Tzotzil and the Tzeltal — live in the state of

Chiapas following the patterns of Mayan life, relatively unchanged since ancient times.

I reached Tuxtla Gutiérrez, a hot, industrial town in the lowlands of Chiapas, by late afternoon. The last bus for San Cristóbal, where I was to meet Catherine, was leaving and I raced to it. She had been traveling near Oaxaca with Roger for the past two weeks, but before she left San Miguel, we had agreed to rendezvous in San Cristóbal on August 8.

I didn't look as I jumped on, but I had flung myself into another world — a world of color and unexpected beauty and an ethereal quality of light. The bus was packed with Quiché Maya, the people of the southern highlands, who were all speaking Quiché, their native tongue. The women, with their sleek black hair and olive complexions, smiled at me. They wore brightly colored cloth with beads and ribbons in their hair and sashes around their waists. The men, in white poncho-like shirts, some with red trim, and small black or straw hats, were more somber, staring straight ahead.

Most of the Indians had come from small villages in the hills to buy goods in town, and they carried with them what they could — sacks of lentils and rice, chickens squawking, dangling upside down, their legs tied together. The Indians whispered to each other in Quiché and pointed at me. I was the only foreigner on the bus, and in my green army pants and an army shirt, some thought I was a soldier. Others just laughed, finding it amusing to see a gringa dressed in this fashion.

The bus was already crowded and I had to stand near the driver for most of the fifty miles up a winding mountain road. As the bus twisted and turned, I hung on tightly. We passed the Indians of Chiapas walking up the road, often with baskets of food or pitchers of water on their heads, each in a colorful costume. Every village has a different costume. I saw Mayans in pink ponchos and in yellow shirts. I stared out the bus window as we climbed in the late afternoon light.

Most of the Indians could speak a broken Spanish and

eventually I made conversation with some of them. I asked a woman seated behind me if she lived in San Cristóbal and she laughed and said she lived in San Juan Chamula, and I should visit her sometime. She sliced a piece of mango for me and I sucked on it. When I said it was good, everyone smiled at me. A man moved his chickens out of the way and invited me to sit on his burlap sack of lentils. I rode the rest of the way, sitting on the sacks of lentils and flour.

San Cristóbal de las Casas is a city of about thirty thousand people. Standing in a high mountain valley, it was named for the Spanish missionary Bartolomé de Las Casas. Las Casas, revolted by the torture and slaughter of the Maya during the conquest — led by the infamous psychopath Pedro de Alvarado — went to Spain to plead the cause of the indigenous peoples. They considered him their protector, and his name was given to this town of arcaded palaces and low, red-tile roofs.

Catherine hadn't checked into La Ciudad Real, our agreed meeting place, but I checked in, assuming she'd be there for dinner. I liked the hotel right away. Its lobby was a beautiful courtyard with a fountain. I was given a windowless room on the first floor at the back of the lobby. It was dark but quiet. The minute I got into the room I collapsed. I had no idea how long I'd slept, but I woke to a complete blackout — there was no electricity. Somehow I changed my clothes and made my way out of my room.

It turned out to be about five-thirty in the morning, and I decided to go for a walk. I did not know where I was going, but I saw Indians in bright-colored costumes making their way through the center of town to a side street, so I followed them. The Mayans of San Cristóbal were heading for market, where there were the vendors of vegetables and fruits, the women who sold handwoven cloth, and others with live rabbits, chickens, baby goats, and lambs. I bought some fruit — bananas and mangoes — which I had for breakfast along with an oily cup of coffee. I walked for a long time among these people and then after a while, feeling tired, I went back to the hotel, hoping to find Catherine.

She was not there when I returned, so I went into my room to rest. It was not long before there was a knock. "Catherine?" I shouted, jumping up and flinging open the door.

A young hotel worker stood there. "Do you need candles? Do you need light?" I said I did and thanked him for thinking of me. He returned with candles and said, "Are you married? Will you invite me to talk to you in your room?"

I sighed. I was not in the mood. "I am waiting for my husband," I told him. "I cannot invite you to my room."

Not one to be slighted, he said, "My name is Chaco. I will come by later. I will bring more candles."

I spent the rest of the morning waiting for Catherine, and when she had not arrived by lunchtime I went to the Na Balom Museum, the House of the Jaguar. Na Balom is the house of Frans Blom, the archaeologist who died here in 1963. He and his wife, Gertrude, spent much of their lives studying the peoples of Chiapas and helping preserve the culture of various indigenous tribes. Gertrude Blom still runs Na Balom as a museum and maintains a foundation for the care of the Lacandon Indians.

The only way to see Na Balom is on a tour, which I signed up for, but it was hopelessly tedious. The guide was clearly a worshiper of Frans Blom, and the tour mainly consisted of a eulogy to the great man.

I found myself drifting away from the group, wandering down a small corridor, until I came upon a large dormitory-type room. I peered inside and saw a man standing there. He had long black hair draped below his shoulders and he wore what looked like a burlap sack. Beside him were a box filled with dead toucans and an enormous bow and quiver. I recognized what the Cherokee Indian had told me to look for — a Lacandon. As I looked in, I heard giggling. A woman, dressed as he, and a small child huddled in a corner.

"Do you speak Spanish?" I asked him.

He smiled, displaying gold teeth. "I have learned that tongue," he said.

"Does your wife speak, and your child?"

He shook his head. "They speak only the language of our people."

"And who are your people?" I asked.

"Lacandon. And who are your people?"

"North Americans," I said. "How did you get here?"

"In a giant bird. They sent me here to give me these teeth." He smiled again so that I could admire his gold teeth. "We come from far away. A jungle I cannot see from here."

"I come from far away as well."

"From where?" he asked.

"I come from New York."

"And where is New York?" he asked.

"In the United States . . ." He looked at me oddly. "In North America."

"Where is North America?" he asked.

I pointed over my head, my arm stretching across the jungle and the high desert, through the arid land south of the Río Grande, across the river and the border, my hand reaching as far as it could reach. "Over there," I said, and he smiled with his gold teeth, pleased to know where my jungle was.

The next day Catherine had still not arrived. I went to the telegraph office. I had inquired there several times before, but this time, after much searching, they found a cable. It read, "Behind schedule, Catherine." I asked if this was all they had received and they said that this was all. No indication of how far she was behind schedule, no sense of when to expect her, no salutation. No love.

I felt empty and unsure here at the tip of Mexico, in the heart of Central America, a woman traveling alone with no idea of what to do next. Some French tourists had told me about a place where you could rent horses. I found the spot, met the owner, who said his name was Abondio, and asked if I could rent a horse for the next day.

"Where do you want to go?" he asked.

I had no idea, but I recalled the nice woman on the bus

who had given me a piece of mango. "San Juan Chamula," I said.

Abondio, who was, I think, about my age, but seemed much older, nodded. He looked weathered and tired, with dark, mottled skin and a forehead with deep creases. "Yes," he said, "the best way to go to Chamula is by horse, but it is not an easy ride."

"I've ridden before," I said.

"Then come at six in the morning and bring something to eat."

I tried to go to bed early, but a knock at the door woke me up. "María, do you want a candle?" He had learned my first name. "María, can I talk to you in your room?" It was the waiter, Chaco, and I told him to go away.

IN MY CHILDHOOD FANTASIES I SAW MYSELF AS AN adventurer, a pioneer, a woman hero. I was an Indian maiden, named White Eagle or Running Deer, who rode a pinto bareback and hunted buffalo, with bow and arrow, at a full gallop. I was very good at bringing my horse right next to the buffalo and making the arrow pierce its heart with one shot. The animals I hunted always came to me and I never caused them pain.

Or I was the only sister of many brothers who ran a ranch. I could pack a rifle and brand a steer as well as any of them. I knew how to use medical supplies and I was also good with herbs. I had a friend who was a squaw and she taught me how to boil sage and antelope ear to cure a wound. Through my friendship with the squaw, my brothers and I lived in peace with the tribes. We traded beef for furs. They came to us when they broke their bones and they cured our fevers when winter came. They protected us from the nomadic tribes of the plains who did not know our purpose there. And when soldiers came to take their land, I convinced my brothers to talk to the soldiers.

I was faith keeper, peacemaker, diviner, matchmaker, interpreter of magical signs. I envisioned myself in wagon trains and tepees, in jungles and exotic desert lands, discovering an unknown species of reptile, blazing trails across virgin terrain.

In my room dolls sat neglected, waiting for me to tend to them, while I studied the wing of a butterfly under a microscope or determined the genus of a local Midwestern rock. When I did play with them, it wasn't to dress or groom them. It was to have them defend the fortress, protect the wagon train, ride shotgun, or be lookout on high ridges.

Their hair came undone, their dresses were disheveled and torn. Once my father complained. He had seen the dolls of my friends and he wanted to know why my dolls weren't pretty and neat. I said that my dolls had more fun.

In the woods near our house I busied myself with the naming of things — plants, creatures, bits of stone. I embarked upon adventures that involved walks along ravines or on the old Indian trails that marked the bluffs of Lake Michigan, where I would hunt or scout or find medicine for my wounded men. While I saw myself living in suburbia, a candidate for a normal life, none of my fantasies ever involved the PTA, mowing lawns, a husband paying bills. I was always riding at a full gallop, papoose strapped to my back, warrior husband waiting on a ridge. Or child at my breast as I led the wagon train across the Cheyenne.

Sometimes at night in my girlhood I would strip in front of a mirror and look at my body. I admired its taut limbs, its incipient roundness. I tried to imagine it in another place at another time. Not another body, but a body in a different set of circumstances. Covered with the scars of battle, scraped with jungle thorns, beloved by a great and compassionate man.

But in most of my fantasies, the men were away and the women had to be brave. The men were off and the women carried on. Often in my life I have been weak and needy, but if I think back, what I have wanted is to be courageous and strong.

WHEN I REACHED THE STABLE AT SIX, ABONDIO HAD the horses saddled and ready to ride. The horse he gave me was black. I had brought some sandwiches and fruit for us. Abondio said he thought we should not go to Chamula. He said there was a festival that day at Zinacantán and that all the Indians would be there — we would find no one in Chamula. So we set out for Zinacantán.

Although I used to ride every Saturday of my life, I hadn't been on a horse for a while, and I felt a stiffness in my legs. I had no idea how long a ride this would be and I could tell that Abondio was trying to decide if I was a greenhorn who did not know what to do or if he could trust me in the saddle. After a while he decided that he could trust me. He said we would take the scenic route, which was a little more treacherous, but I could handle it.

We barely spoke as we rode. Abondio told me his horse was afraid of blue buses. "Only blue ones," he said. After that I don't remember us speaking. In a short while we left the road. We went across fields where women washed their clothes and their long black braids in quiet streams, past fields of cornflowers and marigold and primrose. We rode past women herding sheep and goats. Rams fought on the edges of rocks while foals galloped in the fields.

We entered the high jungle. It was tropical and dense and there was little room to move. Abondio moved ahead of me with a machete, cutting vines where they had closed in on the trail, and I held back, bending down to keep low branches from hitting me in the head. I didn't know where I was going or what I would find. I could be going anywhere and anything might happen. Doubts began to enter my mind as we went deeper into the jungle.

[78]

There were strange noises — shrieks and cries. Abondio said the noises were coming from howler monkeys and brilliant-colored toucans, but we could not see them during the heat of the day because they were in hiding. I kept my gaze on the tops of the trees, but the monkeys, which I longed to see, eluded me. We continued. Lianas scraped against my arms; branches hit me in the face. It began to rain. We took our horses under a tree, but the rain was very heavy and we were immediately drenched. I had brought a poncho along, but by the time I got it on, my jeans, my boots, my clothes, were soaked. My horse was soaked, the saddle. We rode on in the rain.

When the rain stopped, the day turned steamy and our bodies began to sweat beneath our wet things. My skin crawled. Mosquitoes came out. We pulled up our horses and ate a sandwich. I felt the jungle closing in, the damp heat of the day rising. I thought I couldn't breathe. As we moved deeper, it occurred to me that I did not know this man. Anything could happen in the middle of the Mexican jungle, in the middle of nowhere, not far from the Guatemalan border, where there was rumored to be trouble. No one knew where we were. No one would find us. If anything happened to him, I would be lost forever.

I looked at Abondio carefully. He was a silent, hardened man. I had entrusted myself to him through this jungle that had no trail. And he could do anything he wanted to me. But there was a softness to his eyes, a gentle curve to his lips, and I knew he would not harm me. When you travel alone, you learn to read those inner maps. You learn to trust a landscape that is familiar only inside your head. A look in the eyes, the mouth. The way a person moves his hands.

The rain had made the ground muddy and we proceeded with caution. At one point my horse slid on its knees down a slippery embankment. At the next incline, we dismounted and led the horses. And then, after about three hours, when I was wet and stiff and muddy, we emerged from that dense jungle.

We had come to a valley surrounded by jutting cliffs

covered with green, their peaks obscured by a mist. From the heights of the cliffs, I saw what looked like a maypole of colors, living streamers of yellow and blue, of brilliant orange and green, weaving their way down the steep mountain paths until each color wrapped itself into the next color. The indigenous peoples of southern Chiapas, along with their sheep and their goats, wended their way from their mountain villages — wearing their village colors — to this valley where the trails met. They came from Chamula and Tenejapa and other small villages, climbing down the craggy paths on foot, some leading ponies or burros. From the cliff tops they made their way out of the mist.

It seemed as though they were descending from heaven into a valley of light. We stood in silence, watching the Indians, like ghosts of another time, in their silent walk. In the heart of the valley it illumined the trees and the clay road that opened before us. It illumined the procession of the souls down the mountains. Its rays emblazoned the town of Zinacantán, to which we rode like pilgrims to Jerusalem.

Since the festival had stopped because of the rain, Abondio and I were the main attractions as we galloped into town. The musicians were packing up, the food had been put away, the vendors had gone into a local bar to drink. A crowd flocked around us as we dismounted and tied up our horses at a hitching post. I was the only foreigner in sight and no one was quite sure where we'd come from. Guatemala wasn't that far away, and Abondio assured them that we'd come from San Cristóbal.

I asked two women in the crowd for a bathroom and they looked at me as if I were asking for something they had never heard of. They smiled and were nice and finally someone led me to a yard where there was a small wooden shelter. As I walked into the shelter, three pigs ran out of it.

For an hour we strolled through the town, our shoes sloshing in the mud, but then Abondio said it would probably rain again and perhaps we should get back. He apologized for the festival, but I said I didn't mind. I'd seen what I'd come for.

We rode along the muddy slopes and swampy impasses. It began to rain again and I didn't bother with my poncho. I was soaked. Our horses slid and kicked mud and we were covered in filth. It was almost sunset when we left the jungle and the sky was a pale orange. It rained again and this time the rain washed the mud from us.

When the rain ceased, Abondio said we could gallop. The light shimmered down through the broken clouds, into the fields of golden wheat. Women washing in the streams stopped and waved as we rode by.

WHEN I RETURNED I FOUND CATHERINE ASLEEP IN our room. She was surprised to see me, filthy, scratched, covered with mud, and I was stunned to see her. In fact I had practically forgotten about her. Now I was a solitary jungle traveler. I had crossed dangerous terrain and lived to tell about it. I had dealt with rain and bugs and dirt and was not thwarted, but Catherine was traumatized by her bus trip from Oaxaca, which had taken over thirty-six hours. She had sent me a long cable explaining the difficulties, signed love and what have you. When I showed her the cable of three words I'd received, she was dismayed.

I was only half pleased to see her. During the day I had grown accustomed to the idea of making this journey alone, and I was beginning to enjoy my sense of independence. I had it in my mind that I would push on to Palenque in the morning, leaving word for Catherine. But now here she was. She was exhausted and upset and I felt the peace I had achieved on my long ride from the Indian village beginning to crumble.

I told her that I'd been in San Cristóbal for four days and felt ready to go on to the Yucatán to the ruins of Palenque, but she was not ready to go anywhere for a day or so.

Catherine rested the next day while I roamed the city. San Cristóbal at its center is a colonial town, built in the old Spanish style with cobblestone streets, but around its peripheries Indians live in modest dwellings, and in the large market place, which is the heart of the town, they sell their goods. I walked through the market one last time, looking at the handwoven blankets, the silver jewelry, the varieties of spices and strange fruits.

That night as we lay in our twin beds, reading, Catherine said, "I feel anxious about so many things."

I didn't want to discuss this, having just felt very un-anxious about my life for the first time in a while. On the other hand, it seemed she wanted to talk. "You mean, men?"

She nodded. "I mean everything." She was upset about her boyfriend in Seattle who was moving them to a new apart-ment, about Roger, the man she'd been traveling with, about her career. "It's just too much."

"Well, why don't you use this trip to relax?"

"Yes, that's what I'll do."

Just then there was a knock at our door. Chaco appeared for his final attempt. "Mary," he whispered, "do you want a candle? Mary, I want you. I am going to be sad. Don't go tomorrow." Catherine and I fell asleep, laughing into our pillows, with poor Chaco knocking, never understanding why my husband had not arrived.

At six we got to the bus station, which was basically a mud hut at the edge of town where a woman served terrible coffee. Eventually a rickety, dirty bus arrived and we boarded. We found seats near the rear. Suddenly scores of French and German tourists arrived and managed to push themselves on.

We had a twelve-hour ride in a crammed bus with no shocks on a bumpy dirt road that descended into the steamy lowlands of the tropics. A French woman sat on my armrest, her thigh literally in my lap. I wouldn't have minded if she'd asked if she could sit on the armrest, but she just plunked herself down and we spent the entire ride giving each other little nudges and pushes.

We were hot and uncomfortable and I had no idea how we'd make it through the journey into the jungle. At each stop, barkers ran up to the bus, selling Popsicles, warm Cokes, fruit-flavored slush, barbecued corn, and tacos. I was dying for some slush, but we knew the water could be bad, so we settled for warm Cokes. Catherine, who exhibited an impressive capacity for sleeping in unpleasant circumstances, dozed as we drove down to the hot and muddy lowland jungle. I was wedged between her and the French woman sitting in my lap. But I soon forgot my discomfort.

Entering the lowland jungle I confronted a fantasy of my childhood — a world of butterflies, butterflies I had read about in my youth when I belonged to a South American butterfly club. Butterflies I had seen only in the enormous butterfly book my parents had given me or on display at the Field Museum of Natural History in Chicago. Butterflies that in my heart I had never really believed existed, until now.

A blue morpho, that iridescent turquoise-blue butterfly, hovered over fallen fruit. Another flitted through the jungle. The blue morpho, most secretive of butterflies, most private, the butterfly whose life history is unknown. I saw others I recognized. The *Heliconius doris* with its long, narrow wings. A brilliant silver shoemaker with its emerald-green wings. A bamboo page, a common page, a figure-of-eight butterfly, the cobalt-blue and black Nymphalid, the orange Grecian shoemaker. The owl butterfly, the Southern cattle heart, the plain yellow swallowtail.

They were all right there. The ones I had spent years studying, then forgetting. And now they were all here, for me to remember.

At about seven o'clock that evening, exhausted, filthy, disgusted from the ride, we arrived at Palenque. The town was an array of mud and cement houses. Garbage was everywhere, flies were in everything, and people, exhausted from the heat, swung as if drugged from hammocks suspended between burnt-out palms. We clomped through the town and stopped to get some fruit salad. Catherine gently picked three dead flies out of hers and flicked them to the ground. I could not bring myself to eat mine.

She was running short of money and wanted to stay in a

place that would cost us each only a dollar a day. The rooms consisted of straw mats on a dirt floor and I balked at staying there, in the tropical heat, so Catherine agreed to check into a decent hotel here in Palenque if I would stay in a hammock place on Isla Mujeres. At that point I would have agreed to a lobotomy.

We found a hotel near the ruins called the Motel de las Ruinas. The big draw for both of us was its beautiful, gigantic swimming pool filled with sparkling water in which we intended to spend all our free time. For some reason we were given a room with a double bed. We stripped down and jumped in the shower. Catherine went in first and came out screaming. A large toad was tucked in the corner of the stall. I am squeamish about insects and she is terrible with reptiles. I couldn't get it out so we showered with the toad watching.

We lay on the bed, naked, the overhead fan churning away, until we found the energy to go out for dinner. We had seen some sort of a restaurant about a mile down the road and we decided to walk while it was still light, hoping to get a ride back in the dark. As we walked, we listened to the jungle sounds. Shouts, shrieks, screeches, hoots, howls, yells. The road was lined with carcasses. Dead snakes, land crabs, small rodents. A large black spider that looked like a black widow raced in front of us across the road.

It was dark by the time we reached the restaurant, which consisted of a few picnic tables, a dirt floor, and red and green Christmas lights encircling the tables. It also had a baby wild boar named Petunia, who ran around begging for food. Petunia, when fed and contented, rolled over onto her back to get her tummy rubbed. I was surprised to find that the belly of a wild boar is soft as a baby's.

Catherine didn't like Petunia and seemed annoyed at my feeding her. I was nervous about the prospect of having to walk back to the motel in the dark and managed to irritate Catherine by devoting most of the meal to trying to find us a ride. We ate plates of rice and beans, cooked meat and plantains, all of which was good, and drank warm beer. But whenever a new customer appeared, I rushed over to ask about a ride. Eventually an Italian couple on their honeymoon took pity on us. "You poor girls," the woman, who was not much older than us, said. "Wandering alone like this." She clutched the arm of her bespectacled husband at the thought. They lingered over their meal, touching hands, while I rubbed Petunia's belly and Catherine sat in silence. Finally they were ready to leave and they went out of their way to take us home.

NOBODY GOES TO PALENQUE IN MID-AUGUST AND what we were doing there then remains a mystery to me. Perhaps it was just a case of bad planning. But there we were, and we experienced it in its full force. The minute we stepped outside in the morning the heat struck us, bowled us over like a blast furnace. Our jeans, which we'd washed out the night before, were stiff as boards, dry as clay in the morning sun. But my hair never felt dry the entire time I was in Palenque; it was always soaked with sweat. As we walked to the ruins, the people swung in their hammocks, expressionless, barely moving, dead looking, brains boiled. The jungle of Palenque was not like that of the highlands. Here there were no hills, no vistas, no gentle rolling of the land. In Palenque you were at the bottom of a pit of the lowlands, enclosed in a jungle prison. No breeze blew through this hollow. It felt ominous, treacherous, omnivorous, and indifferent, as if it would swallow you with a single gulp. If you stood still for just a moment, vines would engulf you, snakes would poison you, small crawling things would devour you, the air would be stolen from you. And you would be forgotten.

We entered the lost city of Palenque, a city of overgrown trails and crumbled ruins, a mysterious place about which little is known. Once a thriving city, Palenque was abandoned suddenly in the tenth century when all the great Mayan centers were abandoned for reasons unknown. I walked through its main causeways, among its temples and houses and courts where sports were played. I walked through these ruins with steam baths, public toilets with septic tanks, aqueducts, and drainage systems. I tried to imagine the city that had been.

Palenque, whose civilization was concurrent with that of the dawn of civilization in Greece and Egypt, is a place of questions, of things you must accept because no answers are forthcoming. Palenque isn't even its original name. After many years archaeologists have deciphered a date, which translates to A.D. 682; they believe it is the completion date of the first pyramid. But no one can explain those pagoda-like temples reminiscent of those in China or at Angkor Wat in Cambodia. No one knows about Pakal, the prince entombed in an obsidian mask at the bottom of the great pyramid of the same name. He is believed to have been a captive, a prince of another tribe, yet the people of Palenque spent years building him the only pyramid in all of Mexico that is also a tomb.

Catherine and I climbed. We climbed each temple, every pyramid. We descended into the cool, wet depths of the tomb, then rose to see the astrological markings at the observation tower. We saw the entire valley from the observation tower, where the Mayan rulers observed the stars and charted their course and made their calendar — a calendar more accurate than ours. No one knows how they accomplished this, and no one knows why the Mayan people dispersed, leaving their cities and their religious centers centuries before the conquistadors arrived.

I left Catherine and climbed to the top of the Temple of the Sun; I saw the Temple of the Foliated Cross and imagined in the distance people struggling up the hill. Mayans going to their places of worship, dragging boulders, building their temples, stone by stone, painting beautiful pictures on the walls. I saw them fighting back the jungle, futilely pushing it away. I could see them from where I stood, a great, passionate, religious people who had disappeared but for their ruins.

Then I walked into the jungle a little ways. A horde of soldier ants descended a tree. In my path were a red-bellied spider with skinny legs, reminding me of the black widow we thought we'd seen the night before, and butterflies of topaz, amber, turquoise, earth brown. Tigers, monarchs, delicate lace-leafed butterflies, little pearl and azul ones, big yellows and the giant blues — the cobalt-blues — all flew past me. I heard the sounds of strange animals as I made my way through the lush vegetation.

At dusk Catherine and I staggered back to the hotel with only one thought in our minds. We would strip, put on our suits, and take that swim. We walked in silence and I do not recall ever being quite so exhausted. As we approached the hotel, the pool appeared before us, turquoise. We kept walking, but the pool was not so shimmering as it had seemed the day before. As we drew nearer, I did not take my eyes from it. Catherine gaped as well. When we were only twenty feet away, I stopped. "Look," I said.

Catherine nodded. "It's not possible," she said.

We reached the edge of the completely empty swimming pool, the pool which had been full of water the afternoon before but did not have a drop in it now. We rushed to the man who sat in the office drinking a warm Coke, feet on his desk, and he told us that the pool was dirty so they had decided to drain it. We shook our heads in utter disbelief. We went to our room to shower and I felt someone was playing a cruel joke on us — there was no water. We rushed back to the man at the desk. He told us that they'd run out of water. For reasons we've never understood the hotel decided to drain the swimming pool on the same day they ran out of water. "When will you have more water?" Catherine asked.

The man shrugged. "Later," he said.

We went back to our room and lay on the bed, miserable, not speaking. Then we wiped ourselves off with half a dozen Wash 'n Dris each and went to the restaurant where we'd eaten the previous night. Petunia, who seemed to know me now, rolled over on her back to have her stomach rubbed throughout the meal, much to Catherine's annoyance. Eventually the owner came over and sat down. He asked if we liked Palenque and we said we did, but we were very hot and our hotel had no water. "Then you must go to Agua Azul," he said. "It is beautiful. Dozens of waterfalls. Yes, you must go there and swim."

We were lucky that morning. About a hundred people were waiting to push onto the local bus that would take us to Agua Azul, but the ticket taker took pity on Catherine and me. He was a young man of about seventeen with a kind and handsome dark face, warm brown eyes. And he wore pink. He wore a shiny pink shirt with some kind of animal — elephants, I think — all over it, and pink pants. One doesn't normally see a man dressed all in pink. That fact has stayed with me, and always will.

Since we were going all the way to Agua Azul, two hours up the mountain — not just to Egipto or Santa María, the mud and thatch villages along the way — and since we were the only blue-eyed gringas around, the ticket taker got us seats before the local people piled on. Then he opened a window for us and let everyone else board.

There seemed to be no limit to how many people the bus could hold. As many as showed up squeezed on. Mothers clutched screaming babies and pushed and dragged their chickens and goats. Men with machetes stood bleary-eyed in the heat. All had misery in their faces, the pain of drudgery.

The bus climbed and the breeze and the cooler air made everyone feel better. Slowly, as people got off, we felt the terrible heat letting up. The ticket taker in pink joked with us. He asked if Palenque had been hot enough for us. And he said Agua Azul was a beautiful place.

In two hours we reached Agua Azul, with its twenty or so main waterfalls and a series of lesser ones; small pools formed at the bases of some falls, and we could swim in these. Our driver said we'd stay for about two hours, then return. Catherine and I changed into our suits in a small wooden dressing room. A dead tarantula lay on the floor.

I headed for one of those little pools at the base of the falls while Catherine got a beer and started off on a walk. Our bus driver, a very gentle, elderly man with soft gray eyes, sat on the edge of a rock and pointed to a pool near him. He told me this was not a bad place to swim. I eased my way into the icy water and felt the cool go through me. I felt alive, tingly, happy to be in water. I began to swim. I swam out into the pool and back again, but about midway I could feel the current — strong, pulling at me.

Catherine came back. She said she'd seen a large wild boar, drowned, in one of the pools. "Be careful," she said. I looked at where I'd been swimming. The pool where I swam fed into a waterfall that fell about ten yards. It didn't look so treacherous and I wasn't very concerned. Catherine went to make us sandwiches with some vegetables, bread, and cheese we had brought from town. She said she'd be back with lunch.

I went into the water again. A boy had entered the pool and was swimming beside me. I swam out and back a few times, and each time I felt the current at that one place. Finally I decided it was dangerous and that I should not swim all the way across and back. But the boy, flailing about like a puppy, was not a very controlled swimmer, and he was making his way back and forth well beyond the place where I was stopping. I remember thinking to myself, I should tell him that the current is very strong. I should say something. But I did not. I didn't want to pry or bother him. He must know what he is doing, I told myself. Then Catherine called me for lunch.

I hoisted myself out of the water. As I walked toward her, my body felt cool for the first time in days and I smiled. I felt incredibly vigorous and content as Catherine held a sandwich out to me. Hungry and ready to eat, I reached for it, but our hands never connected. Her face changed from one of greeting to one of stunned horror. Her mouth opened, but all she could do was point to the place where I had been swimming.

From the corner of my eye I saw the boy who had been

swimming next to me. He seemed to be riding one of those carnival watersled rides because he was practically sitting up and the current was just taking him along. I could see his face now and he looked familiar to me, like an old acquaintance you meet after many years but cannot quite place.

He was silent. That is what I remember most. The silence. He never screamed or shouted or cried for help. His face had the concentration of a good student taking an important exam. When he got to the falls, he twisted his body, trying to grab onto a branch, and then he was gone without a sound. Suddenly we were both screaming and pointing at nothing, at nothing at all except the rush of water.

The Mexicans did not believe us. They said no boy was missing. No one was missing anyone, but we were hysterical. "Someone went over that fall," we told them. At the same time I could not help thinking how I had done nothing. How that boy had been swimming near me and I had thought to say something and had said nothing. And then I thought how close it had come to being me. If I had gone out just a little farther, it would have been me.

Then our bus driver came toward us slowly, eyes glassy. He clasped in his hands the pink shirt and pink pants of the ticket taker, who had given us our seats. He said nothing. He simply held out the boy's clothes.

It took a while, but a search party was organized. About a dozen young Mexican men stripped down to their shorts and with sticks went to the base of the falls, where they formed a line. We sat on the bank over the falls, watching. Catherine seemed nervous and soon began pacing. But I sat, transfixed, never taking my eyes off the search party. I watched the bodies of young men, bodies so perfect and beautiful that I wanted to touch them as they bent over the water and put their faces in, like divers after mother-of-pearl. They walked and probed as I sat and waited, but no body was found.

A Mexican who seemed to be in charge came over to us. "He is at the bottom of the falls. It has happened here before.

The body will be trapped there forever." The bus driver was in tears now. He knew the boy and his family well. The Mexican shrugged. "We'll keep looking," he said. They searched for two hours while we waited on the bank.

Finally the driver patted me on the shoulder. "Let's go," he said.

"I should have done something," I said to Catherine as we got on the bus. "When we were swimming, I should have said something."

"Be grateful it wasn't you," she said.

"I am, but I should have done something."

Catherine opened up a copy of *Tropic of Cancer* and read all the way back to Palenque. I tried to talk to her, but she would not discuss the incident with me. She just said, "It wasn't your fault. It was an accident, so forget it."

CATCHING THE NIGHT TRAIN TO MÉRIDA FROM Palenque is a little like trying to escape from Casablanca during World War II. Hundreds of campesinos ran about us, fighting to get tickets, pushing in line. Others sat on sacks of rice and potatoes, looking dumbfounded and confused. Some had chickens, goats, lambs, all tied by the feet and struggling to get away. Mayan Indians wandered about. Tourists rushed by, trying to procure nonexistent first-class tickets.

Catherine and I had both wanted to leave Palenque after the day at Agua Azul, but now at the train station, I felt dazed and let Catherine take care of things. I sat on our luggage, as if I were not even there. Eventually Catherine returned, displaying two first-class tickets. I have no idea how she got these. I had anticipated spending the night on a sack of flour, but somehow she had managed this. She said we were guaranteed seats, even though they weren't reserved. I needed her to take over at this moment in our trip and I was appreciative.

The train pulled in about an hour later and everyone piled on. The first-class compartment was full, except for four seats that two very fat Mexicans were occupying. They were lying down, sprawled out. They were obviously friends of the conductor because he refused to look at their tickets or make them sit up. Catherine found a seat right away, but there was none for me. I felt completely on edge and out of sorts. I asked her what I should do and she said I should wait and eventually there would be one.

I went between cars and began to cry. I probably needed to do so, but I felt foolish and childish. After a while Catherine came to find me. She told me to pull myself together and she managed to talk the conductor — actually I think she may have bribed him — into getting me a seat. At about one in the morning we found two together. Catherine, as usual, fell asleep immediately, and slept the whole night through. I sat upright, staring out the window. I struggled to get comfortable but in the end gave up. I watched the Yucatán go past as the train sped through the dark.

The Yucatán-Petén peninsula is a single great limestone shelf that rises up into the blue waters of the Gulf of Mexico, which borders the peninsula on the west and north; its eastern shores, lined with reefs, face the Caribbean Sea. As we moved north to the Yucatán in daylight, the landscape altered, the world changed. We had left the highlands and the tropical lowlands. The world became flat, the jungle receded. We came out into the light.

The goal of our journey, its true direction, had been to travel from the jungle to the sea, and I wasn't sorry to leave the jungle behind. As we headed toward the coast, the heaviness of the landlocked lifted from me. We entered the coastal region and I seemed to wake from a bad dream. Everything felt more normal, and were it not for the houses and the people, it would have been almost banal. I saw giant thatched huts like beehives, some on stilts. Mayan women in perfectly white, clean, embroidered dresses stood in front of their houses with their children. It was a world of whiteness, of cleanliness, and of exotic beauty. In Campeche, Mayan women boarded the train and sold delicious sweet coffee and sponge cake.

We reached Mérida by midmorning and settled into a small, comfortable guest house. Mérida is an incredibly peaceful city of color, trade, and Mayan influence. The houses are painted in pale pastels. I learned that the average murder rate in this city of almost three hundred thousand is one a year, and somehow I found this comforting.

Catherine said she wanted to be alone and I left her for a while to stroll the markets of Mérida. I admired the colors of spices, curries and cumins, cayenne, green spices, gray and black flour. Everything had a remarkable smell. I could have been in the bazaars of Jerusalem or Marrakesh. City blocks of chickens and ducks and piglets. Throats being cut before my eyes. Mayan women are beautiful with their pale brown skin and high cheekbones, their jet-black hair and their characteristic noses, which hook down. The noses are a distinctive trait and it amazed me to see the same profiles I'd admired on the images carved in stone at the ruins of Palenque.

The women tried to sell me bracelets of silver, earrings of gold. Small idols, supposedly originals from Mayan ruins. These I knew better than to bargain for. What I was tempted to buy were the giant live beetles, bigger than silver dollars, decorated with paint and rhinestones and little leashes around their necks, being sold as pets. They were dressed as cowboys with small hats, boots on their legs, soldiers in camouflage, and women of the night, with long eyelashes and pink satiny skirts. One woman had these beetles covering her arms, crawling all over her. I had no idea what I'd do with a pet beetle in my travels, so I resisted and kept going.

I bought myself a hammock, some deerskin sandals, a *guayabera* (a man's short-sleeve shirt), and a beautiful Mayan blouse. I visited public buildings famous for their murals depicting the conquest, the period of colonial rule, and then the revolution and the casting off of the conquistadors. The Mayan people are clearly proud of their revolutionary zeal and the fact that, compared to their northern counterparts, who intermarried with the Spanish, their race has remained pure.

When I returned, Catherine was preparing to head for the ruins of Uxmal. The heat of the day was becoming unbearable and I couldn't stand the thought of boarding another bus and riding some sixty miles. But in a way it seemed we just couldn't stop. "Why don't we go tomorrow?" I suggested, but Catherine already had on her small pack. "You can stay here if you like," she said. But I knew I couldn't stay there alone. A momentum had entered our journey. Something had happened to us since Agua Azul and we were like women being chased.

IN A FEW DAYS WE WERE READY TO GO TO THE SEA, and we caught an early afternoon bus to Puerto Juárez, which we reached in time to miss the last ferry to Isla Mujeres. We would have to spend the night in Puerto Juárez, something we had no desire to do. Puerto Juárez only exists as a place to get the ferry to Isla Mujeres. For accommodations, we had two choices. We could stay in a fairly expensive hotel (about seven dollars a night, including dinner). Or for about a dollar we could rent a giant tin box with no ventilation, boiling hot inside, like an Indian sweatbox used for ritual cleansing.

Catherine opted for the tin box, as I knew she would, but I refused, reiterating my promise to sleep at the Isla Mujeres hammock place she had her heart set on. We stayed in a hotel across the way on what was becoming our usual sliding scale — I paid about two thirds. Years later when Catherine actually had money and suggested we do away with the sliding scale, I found I could not do it. It made me as uncomfortable as when one of my high school teachers suggested we call him by his first name.

At about eight-thirty in the morning we arrived at the ferry dock to check the schedule. The man who sold tickets sat beneath a sign that listed the departure hours: 9:00, 11:00, 13:00, 16:00. But when we asked him if the boats would be running on schedule, he said we'd just missed the morning ferry — it had sailed at eight — and we would have to wait until noon and, after that, until three o'clock.

Catherine began to lose her temper. "How is it possible that the morning ferry sailed when the sign says nine o'clock?"

"It left at eight." He shrugged.

"So why don't you change your sign to read 'eight'?"

I told her to sit down and have a cup of coffee while I wandered over to the dock, where I saw passengers boarding a ferry. I asked the captain which island he was going to and he said Isla Mujeres, in five minutes. He told me the ferries were shuttles and continuous all day long, which was not what the ticket seller or his sign said. I raced back, got Catherine, and a moment later we were on the ferry as it sailed to Isla Mujeres, dolphins jumping in our wake.

The hammock room at the Poc-Na had twelve hammocks — six slung high and six slung low — with virtually no protection from the outside world. The roof consisted of wooden slats that didn't quite come together, and I prayed it wouldn't rain. The sides of the building were wooden louvers, open to the outside, without screens. I thought it would be breezy at night, but during the heat of the day, as I stuffed my things into my locker, it must have been about 110 degrees. The room smelled as if small creatures had died in the walls.

Catherine wanted to go off on her own to write letters and read. She had been preoccupied and moody for days and I thought it best to let her be alone. I went to the telegraph office and cabled Alejandro to say I'd be back in three or four days. After sending the cable, I rented snorkel gear at the Poc-Na and was told there was good snorkeling up the beach. I walked about a mile until I came to a place where other snorkelers were preparing to dive.

I put on my gear and went in. A school of thousands of fish surrounded the mouth of a turquoise cave and I dove in and out among the fish. The current was not terribly strong and I could swim into the turquoise cave a little ways without fear of being dashed into the rocks. Then I swam back among the school of fish.

I swam across the reef, across oscillating sea grass reaching for me in that warm Caribbean sea. On the reef I swam with the tropical fish. Angelfish and gourami, blue jacks and a fish that looked like a Picasso plate. I swam farther across the reef and suddenly found myself in shallow water over a bed of sea urchins, their poisonous spines extended. The water distorted the distance and I could not tell if the spines were inches or several feet away. Urchin spines, once they prick you, work their way into your skin. If you get spines in your foot, they can come out of your arm or your face. They can fester and emerge anywhere. I had to get off that reef and away from the urchins.

I turned and swam and found myself at the edge of the reef, overlooking the great expanse of ocean, a basin of darkness, of nothing at all. That dark void before me terrified me as nothing else has. I turned to the reef, to the urchins, to what was known, and floated over them, my eyes closed, back to shore.

That night I tried to sleep in the rope hammock, but my skin, burned and glistening, rubbed against the bristling ropes. Every inch of me stung as if I'd been whipped. The twelve hammocks swayed as if in the galley of a slave ship. Mosquito coils smoked in these rooms where no breeze blew off the sea, where the stifling heat was well over ninety degrees. I tried to get comfortable, finding a way to pull the sheet around me, the pillow under me, to keep my burning skin from rubbing against the rope.

A Norwegian girl shouted in her sleep in accented English, "Hurry up, come. Help." Someone down the row farted. A man above me dangled over the edge of his hammock, threatening to fall. His mouth opened and closed as he snored. Someone panted as if making love. How could anyone touch in this heat? A whimpering sound came from the direction of Catherine's hammock. I looked over. Tears ran down her cheeks. "Are you all right?" I whispered.

I don't know if she heard me, but she turned her face to the wall. I thought I should do something but also felt it was best to leave her alone. I spent the night watching the almost naked bodies, laminated with rope marks, toss and rise and rock.

In the morning Catherine sipped coffee, her duffel at her side. She looked drained, her eyes swollen as if she hadn't slept all night. "You're up early," I said, as she was normally a late sleeper.

"I'm going."

I took a sip of her coffee. "To the beach?"

"No, to California."

I felt as if we hadn't stopped for a moment, but now she was ready to leave. She said she wanted to get back. Her decision seemed abrupt and startled me, but I can't say I was displeased. I had grown weary of the tension between us and wanted to be on my own. I told her I would stay a few more days.

Before she left, we took a walk and she said, "Look, this isn't a very good time for me and I don't think it's a very good time for you. A lot of bad things are happening with me now. I've got this boyfriend in Seattle who's just moved all our stuff to Eugene and I don't think he's right for me. Roger should be back in San Francisco and he wants me to move down there with him. I don't know what I'm going to do," she went on. "I need some time alone. We're not getting along very well. I think we should just go our separate ways."

I agreed this was the best thing. Then I loaned her the seventy-five dollars she needed to get home and assumed I'd never hear from her again, though a check and a letter would be awaiting me upon my return.

I could no longer stand the heat in the hammock room and so that night I took the hammock I'd purchased in Mérida and went to the beach. I had visited several of the beaches and there was one, not far from the Poc-Na, that was desolate and pristine.

It was a beautiful night as I made my way along a dark,

sandy inlet. When I reached the shore, I found two palmettos that were just the right distance apart and I tied my hammock to them with a strong double hitch. I stretched out on my back and watched as a full moon came up. There was a slight breeze and the mosquitoes weren't too bad and I lay there listening to the waves of the warm, shallow water lap the shore and watching the bright orange moon come up over the sea.

On an impulse, I took off my clothes and folded them on the hammock. Standing naked, my feet in the cool sand, I walked to the sea. My skin felt cool as I stood alone, watching the shadow of my body flickering in the golden stream of moonlight stretching before me. I felt as if I could enter that stream and swim to America, to Africa, to the end of the world.

I walked into the water. The sand beneath my toes was silken, the water warm. I walked into the water as if into a baptismal. My feet disappeared into the blackness, my toes dug deeper into the sand. My feet were gone, my legs to the knees. At the edge of the Caribbean, on an isolated strip of beach, everything came back to me. Everything that had ever happened to me and to my body. It all came back there. And when I could stand the infusion of memory no longer, I dove in. I swam in the warm salt water, under the light of the moon. Water held me.

Women remember. Our bodies remember. Every part of us remembers everything that has ever happened. Every touch, every feel, everything is there in our skin, ready to be awakened, revived. I swam in the sea. Salt water cradled me, washing over all I had ever felt. I swam without fear in the line of moonlight radiating on the surface of the sea. The water entered me and I could not tell where my body stopped and the sea began. My body was gone, but all the remembering was there.

I stood up in the water and shook as a dog does. Then, heading toward my hammock, I spotted two figures stirring on the dunes. I caught only a glimpse of their movement at first, but then I saw them. With their heads barely tucked beneath the dune, they were watching me. "What are you doing?" I shouted. I wondered how long they had been watching me and suddenly I was afraid. I covered my breasts with my hands. They were moving along the edge of the dune and my clothing was far up the beach. The men began running in my direction and I turned and fled.

I ran back into the water and dove. It was shallow and I swam slowly under the surface. I thought how easy it would be for them to pluck me from the sea. I kept swimming up the shore, away from the place in the moonlight I had found, oblivious of the urchins, the barracuda, the night eaters, the reaching fingers of jellyfish. I swam into the darkest water of all and stayed there, until they were gone.

4

IN THE CITY

LYING MIDWAY BETWEEN THE PACIFIC OCEAN AND the Gulf of Mexico and in the center of an area of great fertility is a valley forty miles wide and sixty miles long. Rising seven thousand feet above sea level, this valley is flanked on the southwest by Mount Ajusco and on the southeast by two other volcanoes — Popocatépetl, named for a warrior, and Ixtaccíhuatl, named for the Aztec princess who loved him and refused to outlive him. With fertile fields, shallow lakes, plentiful water, a temperate climate, and a cornucopia of tropical fruits, this valley — formerly called Anáhuac — is the Valley of Mexico. It is where the great Aztec Empire was based; it is what Cortés sought to conquer.

Mexico City is a city with a secret, and to live here requires both imagination and will. It is like a person who seems incredibly disheveled but whose core, if you dig deep enough, is ordered, sure, and compelled by belief. What you see when you arrive in this smog-ridden, traffic-heavy city of eighteen million people — many of whom are unemployed peasants from the campos who haven't yet made it to the border — will make you crazy. But its secret is this: beneath its poverty, its filth, its damaged people, another reality exists.

Imagine that the avenue you are riding down, the traffic jam you are sitting in, is the site of what was once a remarkable courseway of roads and lakes and bridges and floating gardens and temples in a perfect, dry, blue valley. A city intended to be a valley for the gods, a paradise, a place of purity and holiness and simplicity, like Jerusalem or Delphi, Machu Picchu or Shangri-La.

Before becoming the first conquistador, Hernando Cortés

lived in the Spanish colony of Cuba. He was extremely fond of cards, gambling, and women. But then, at the age of thirty-three, this ne'er-do-well Romeo somehow changed into a Christian soldier. In 1519, on August 15, which is the feast of the Assumption of the Mother of God, Cortés burned his boats so that there was no turning back and marched from the coast toward the mythical city that had been described to him by the natives. *"México, México,"* the natives had said, pointing north, and as Bernal Díaz described it, they marched toward the city, having no idea what "México" was.

Weeks later, when Cortés, a white man in armor on a horse, rode into the city of Móctezuma, he was greeted with open arms, for he had fulfilled one of the prophecies of Aztec legend — a shimmering white creature, half man and half horse, would arrive, and he would be their god. Cortés was treated as deliverer and beloved guest for over a year.

When Cortés left the Aztec capital of Tenochtitlán, he placed Pedro de Alvarado in command of the city. Alvarado was a handsome young captain reported to be of extremely erratic behavior. He might be laughing one moment, then throwing a violent fit the next. What happened while Cortés was away will never be known for certain. But according to Aztec account, when Cortés left, Alvarado gave the Aztec priests permission to prepare a traditional feast for their god, Huitzilopochtli, in which human hearts would be sacrificed. While the Aztecs were performing their rituals, Alvarado's men attacked. Spanish soldiers sprang into the plaza in front of the temple pyramids, butchered the unarmed worshipers, looted jewelry from the dead, and mutilated the corpses.

Cortés and his men returned, fighting their way back into the city. Alvarado claimed to have launched a pre-emptive attack, having intercepted a communiqué indicating that the Aztecs planned to attack the Spanish. But apparently Cortés did not believe Alvarado, for he declared his behavior that of a madman.

After the attack the Aztecs were not so docile, and war

was inevitable. Eventually the Spaniards conquered. They razed Tenochtitlán and they hung Móctezuma, the great ruler who had greeted them with open arms. On the ruins of the great Aztec capital they constructed a new city; today it is called Mexico City.

The past repeats itself. History builds layer upon layer. Mexico City is an archaeologist's dream and an urban planner's nightmare. If you try to dig a subway tunnel or excavate for a new building, you will come across the ruins of the Temple Major or of a monument to Quetzalcóatl. The Spaniards built their new city — their enormous colonial churches and houses of justice — directly on top of the Aztec temples and houses they destroyed.

What remains in Mexico today, four hundred years after its past was buried, is an incompatible mix of cultures — Spanish, French, United States, and indigenous Mesoamerican. The conquistadors, through genocide, cultural destruction, and miscegenation, managed to obliterate the great empires of North and South America: the Incas, the Mayas, the Aztecs, and the North American tribes. But in Mexico it is still all there — beneath the city the Spaniards built. The language, the culture, the artwork, the sense of time, the spiritual beliefs, the connections to earth and sky, remain beneath the structure of Western values and Christianity. It is all there.

ALEJANDRO HAD GIVEN ME THE KEYS TO HIS APARTment, saying I could stay with him in Mexico City when I returned. I had been looking forward to seeing him and did not feel in a hurry to return to San Miguel. When I arrived, I found his building, a nondescript apartment complex not far from the Paseo de la Reforma and the center of things, and let myself in. I stood for the first time in this ground-floor apartment, a dark one-bedroom whose two windows looked into an enclosed, lifeless courtyard. It was a Saturday and I was a day late. There was no note for me, no sign of when Alejandro would be back. I couldn't find much to eat in the icebox, which surprised me. When Alejandro visited me in San Miguel, he always made me some soup or rice and beans.

I examined the decor. Brocade furniture covered with sheets and plastic slipcovers, rococo lamps with scenes of maidens and nymphs, one horrible painting of a large-eyed woman with her hand pressed over her mouth. A yellow television and many books, a rather extensive library, in fact, which included Hemingway and Bellow, each volume wrapped in a carefully labeled brown paper cover. The library aside, I had no idea how I would be able to spend time here, but I decided to relax until Alejandro got home.

An hour later the door opened and a strange woman with a suitcase walked in. She was extremely fat and ugly with a large black mole on her cheek and a rather mean, unfriendly face. She looked at me oddly. I could see immediately that she knew who I was but had not expected to find me, and that she was clearly displeased with my presence. I said hello as politely as I could and introduced myself. She said she was Alejandro's stepmother. Then she turned on the yellow television and plunked herself down on the sofa in front of a Mexican soap opera.

I sat down beside her. Someone named Rosario stood at an ironing board, sobbing because her father was in a fight with her brother who hated her boyfriend who'd gotten her pregnant. The boyfriend had disappeared and foul play was suspected, and Rosario, who was about to have her baby, wanted to kill herself.

After a while Alejandro arrived and he looked more than surprised to see me. "María," he said, "what are you doing here?"

"I cabled to say I'd be back yesterday."

Alejandro shrugged. "Well, this is Mexico." My cable had never arrived.

Alejandro quickly perceived that the situation was not a good one, and soon the stepmother began crying, yelling, and packing up all of her things. She was throwing dishes into a box, grabbing her coffee pot. I went into the bedroom and tried to figure out what was going on, but she was speaking very quickly and shouting obscenities I did not understand.

After a while Alejandro came in. He explained to me that the woman he'd lived with for the past two and a half years, Angelita, was the stepmother's younger sister. He told me that Marta, the stepmother, came from a gigantic family of about a million children and that she was the ugliest and the fattest, that her rather beautiful younger sister had wanted to marry Alejandro, and that my presence in the apartment was causing a family crisis.

On weekends, Marta, who taught social studies, lived with Alejandro's father in San Luis Potosí, seven hours north of Mexico City. Three years before, Marta and Alejandro's father had left Mexico City, and Marta was still waiting for her school transfer. Her horrible life consisted of taking the bus every Sunday to Mexico City so she could teach and returning to San Luis Potosí every Thursday afternoon. It was, he told me, no life, and he let her stay with him and sleep on his couch.

After telling me this, Alejandro digressed and spoke to me about his mother. "You see, she was very beautiful," he explained. "And after her my father did not want to have to deal with a beautiful woman." He spoke wistfully, with great sadness in his voice.

I was not prepared for the presence of an angry stepmother on a sofa in front of a yellow TV so I offered to leave, but he said no. He went back to the living room and they talked for hours, it seemed, while I read the *Popol Vuh*, the Mayan book of creation. I contemplated the interconnection between time and reality. The theory of being — pantheism. I saw spirits in animals, in inanimate things. I knew that what I needed now in my life, more than anything, was a different relation to time. I needed to put myself on Indian time. Not where hours or minutes mattered, but where I would look at the bigger picture — life in relation to destiny.

I was depressed and unhappy to be back from my journey, and I thought about how I could be somewhere on a beach in the Caribbean rather than in these dreary rooms. I heard a little more shouting, then quiet. Finally Alejandro returned to the bedroom and said that it was all right. She would accept me and I could stay in the apartment with them.

Alejandro loved to do housework. He liked to get down on his knees and scrub the floor. He liked the feel of the rags and the soap, the swoosh of water, the slippery floor beneath him. After the floors he would go to market and spend the rest of the day making *chiles rellenos*, stuffing chili peppers with ground nuts and raisins, wrapping them in a fine egg-white batter.

In that dark, dingy apartment, in that tiny, miserable kitchen, he would do the wash. He'd put a washboard in the sink and wash by hand sheets, blue jeans, underwear (including mine), all his shirts. He'd hang them up on a line that ran through a small outdoor corridor leading to the apartment. And when they were dry, he'd iron. He'd spend hours gliding the iron across cloth, and anyone could see that this man loved the feel of warm iron pressing on cloth, the disappearance of wrinkles, the look of a folded pile of clothes.

On weekends I would sit in a chair nearby, reading and watching him. I had never seen any man, let alone one from his culture, so involved in domestic duties. "Why are you doing all of this?" I would ask.

"Someone has to," he'd say.

"Did your mother teach you?"

He'd wave his hand as if the mere mention of his mother were an anathema to him. "I learned out of necessity," he said. "And now I like it."

He never really wanted my help, though I always offered it. He wanted to cook, clean, wash, scrub, and iron. He knew how to make Aztec soups with avocado and squash blossoms, how to buy the freshest chicken. He spent hours cleaning shrimp. I'd say, "Should I make dinner tonight?" or "Do you want me to go to market?" And he'd reply, "No, let me take care of you." And I always did.

Alejandro wanted to take me to Teotihuacán, the Aztec ceremonial site on the great plain. "There are things you must know," he told me, "if you are to understand where you are." We took a bus for about an hour on that hot afternoon. As we rode, he pointed out to me the twin volcanoes, Popocatépetl and Ixtaccíhuatl. Of the latter he said, "You see, her shape is the body of a woman lying down. It is said that when her warrior died, she lay on the earth and died and that is what became of her."

Teotihuacán was the center built to Quetzalcóatl, a legendary figure in transition from man to god. A Toltec king named Quetzalcóatl may have existed, but in Toltec mythology and throughout the Mesoamerican world, Quetzalcóatl assumed a stature like that of the Buddha — man in the process of becoming divine.

The Aztecs, who ruled this plain at the time of the conquest, worshiped two gods, each with his own set of priests. Huitzilopochtli, god of the sun and war, did battle with Quetzalcóatl, god of culture and the west. It was here at Teotihuacán, beneath the volcanic lovers, that male and female principle struggled. It was here that the plumed serpent came to represent man attempting to rise to something divine while his aggression and ego pull him down.

At the top of the Pyramid of the Sun, Alejandro pounded on his chest. "I am an Aztec," he said, "*ciento por ciento.* One hundred percent. Everything I am comes from here, from this place. The history of my people has been a history of conquest, of intervention, of a struggle to survive. We have been destroyed, our race defiled." He stared straight ahead as he talked. The wind blew his hair back. His sharply formed features grew more defined. His intensity rose. "You see all these tourists, all these visitors running around. Gringos mainly. No matter how hard we try, Mexico can never be Mexico. We had a revolution and got rid of the Spanish. Now we have the United States. No matter how hard we try, it will never be enough. We will always feel inferior. We will never do enough. We will never catch up. The U.S. is always there, making us feel we are not good enough."

"Don't forget I am a *norteamericana,*" I said. I had learned to make that distinction south of the border, for all Latins call themselves Americans.

"Yes, you are a norteamericana. I suppose I will never be good enough for you, will I?"

I wasn't sure what to think of this, and I was afraid to ask. "Don't be ridiculous," I replied. "You are already good enough for me."

He sighed. "That's not what I mean." He grew sullen and morose and after a while wanted to leave.

I HATED THE PLACE WHERE HE LIVED I COULD NOT help it, but it was a dungeon to me and I was a prisoner there. I tried to like it. I bought flowers and baskets of fruit. I tried to brighten it with small pictures purchased from street merchants. But we were living in a practically windowless apartment in a city in which I knew almost no one but Alejandro.

Every day when Alejandro went to work, I was left alone. I'd sit on the double bed, in a T-shirt and shorts, and immerse myself in death. I read everything I could about Mexico. Malcolm Lowry, D. H. Lawrence's *The Plumed Serpent*, Octavio Paz, Juan Rulfo, Mayan books on death imagery, explanations about Day of the Dead. You could not know Mexico, it seemed to me, without knowing death. Some days I'd work at the Benjamin Franklin Library or I'd go to the National Museum of Anthropology. But mainly I stayed in. I stayed in and read what I felt I needed to know.

In the evenings we went out. "It's not good for you to stay inside like this," he insisted, and he would make plans for us to have dinner with his brother, Ruben, and his wife, a truly awful woman whom Ruben had gotten pregnant. Ruben stayed with Margarita only because of their daughter, Alicia. Alicia was three and she had a burn scar that ran from her neck down her torso. Margarita had left her near the stove one day with a pot of boiling water. Only a miracle had saved her face from a terrible burn. Ruben hated Margarita with a passion equal only to that with which he loved his daughter. He adored this child and I could tell how much it pained him every time she was undressed and he could see her scar.

Some evenings we went to the club where Ruben played

alto sax. He was a very attractive person and it always made me sad to see the terrible things that had befallen him. Whenever Alejandro and I spent the evening with him, we came home depressed.

Other evenings we went out with Carlos, the person Alejandro had been with the night I met him. Carlos and Alejandro, it turned out, were partners in a clothing store, and they often had business to discuss. Carlos was jovial and liked to go drinking, and sometimes all three of us would go to Ruben's club. When we did this, Alejandro would get a little drunk and dance. His friends called him Alejandro Travolta. When the music started, he couldn't sit still. He'd grab me by the hand and pull me to the floor. He knew just how to spin and guide me along. On the dance floor he knew when to clasp me to him and when to let go. Once he got going, he could dance until dawn.

ONE NIGHT I WENT TO A PUBLIC PHONE AND CALLED a woman. I'd met in a gallery. We had spoken briefly and she'd suggested I give her a call sometime. I phoned Mrs. Delano, and we agreed to meet at a café where there was a small exhibit of her paintings. Then she would take us to her house for dinner. I asked if I could bring Alejandro along and she said, "By all means." But when we met at the café, it became clear to me within moments that she was uncomfortable.

We ordered tea and tried to admire her paintings which hung on the wall of the café. Mrs. Delano, who had survived the concentration camps in Germany, was a painter of fairly poor paintings depicting Jewish life throughout the ages. I found them without imagination or interest to me, though it was clear that Mrs. Delano thought of herself as the female Chagall.

As she showed us her work, it seemed she could not look Alejandro in the eye. Indeed she acted as if he were not there at all. She also kept running back and forth to the telephone. When we sat down to our tea, she began to tell us how her cook had suddenly taken ill and we could not go to her home for dinner. Instead she said she'd take us nearby for a sandwich.

Her switch from hospitality to detachment was startling and finally I asked her, "Is anything wrong? I mean, is something bothering you?" She paused and then told us what was on her mind. She told Alejandro that he should leave me, that he had to think about what my parents would say. I told her that Alejandro and I were friends and that my mother would be pleased for me to have friends of different cultures.

Later when I went into the bathroom, Mrs. Delano followed me. She said, "You are making a mistake. I have friends who are Mexicans as well, but they are fair, not dark." Fair, she told me, like us. Alejandro, she said, was of a very humble background. I told her I knew that. It was, in part, what I liked about him.

But she went on. "I was going to have you both to dinner but my father would have hit the ceiling if I'd brought a pure Mexican home. He would not have allowed it." I could see I had miscalculated this woman and I was more than willing to leave, but Mrs. Delano had other things to say about Mexicans. She told me that all the beggars in the city were really gypsies and thieves who didn't work because they were lazy. She said there was plenty of work to be had, but Mexicans wanted to do nothing all day. It was important to distinguish the different kinds of Mexicans, she said. "The ones of European origin, they are a different breed."

Later when she drove us back to the Zona Rosa, she wore her gloves. "I keep my gloves on," she said, "so that no one can steal the rings off my fingers when I stop at stoplights."

When we got back to the apartment, Alejandro was furious. "So," he said, "is this what your race is like?" referring to my Jewish background.

"You sound as racist as she does."

"What else did she say to you?" he asked me. "What did she say when she followed you into the bathroom?"

"She's a stupid person," I said, "forget it." But he wouldn't relent so finally I told him. "Look," I said, "I don't feel the way she does. I wouldn't be here if I did, so let's drop it."

He left the apartment in a huff and brought back a six-pack of beer. He sat down in front of the yellow television, something I'd never seen him do. After a while he said, "Is that why you won't marry me, María, because I'm dark?"

"Marry you? Alejandro, I really care for you, but marriage has never been an issue . . ."

"For you maybe, but what about for me?" He spent the rest of the night sulking. "What am I supposed to do when you're gone?" he asked. When he went to get his fifth beer, I tried to take it out of his hand, but he walked away. "I don't want to hurt you," I called. He shook his head. He said it was already too late.

The next day as Alejandro was leaving for work, he said, "If you want to go to San Miguel, if you'd be happier there, then you should go."

We hadn't really discussed San Miguel. It is odd how you can miss a place, how it can gnaw at you somewhere in the back of your mind, and yet you aren't really aware of it. But now, as he said this, I realized how much I wanted to be there. How much I missed Lupe and the children, and I wondered how it was that I could have stayed away so long. "I'll think about it."

"I won't be angry," he said. "If that's best for you, you should go."

After he left I sat on the bed, thinking about what I wanted to do. At that moment I wanted a friend in Mexico City, someone to talk to. I thought I should take a walk and think things through. Instead, I sat and sat. I sat on the bed, thinking, until the bed began to move. The mattress pitched and rolled and I held on as if I were in a white-water raft. The room shifted. Lamps swayed and the furniture rearranged itself. I did not know what to do, so I ran from the house. I didn't think about anything except leaving. Outside the ground still shifted, the buildings rocked. And then it stopped. Around me people were staring. Some laughed, wiping their brows. When it was over, I realized I was wearing almost nothing. I went back inside.

I DECIDED IT WAS TIME FOR ME TO GO TO SAN Miguel. We went out for a movie and dinner and I told him over dinner that I planned to leave the next day. He said he thought it was a good idea. We were walking home at about one in the morning, both feeling very subdued, when suddenly we heard the screech of brakes, the shattering of glass across Paseo de la Reforma, and when we looked up, we saw that several cars had crashed into one another.

I didn't want to investigate, but Alejandro said, "Perhaps there is something we can do." When we got to the scene of the accident, two women lay sprawled on the ground, one of them crying. "You go," I told him. "I'll stay here." Alejandro made his way through the crowd and a few moments later he came back. Grabbing me by the arm, he pulled me toward the women. "They are North American. They don't speak any Spanish. You have to help."

I reached the women and knelt down. "I am American," I said. "Can I help you?"

The older woman grabbed me. "Oh, thank God, thank God, there is someone we can talk to." She was sobbing hysterically. The younger woman, who seemed to be not as badly injured, told me that she was traveling with her mother. They were Mexican-Americans from San Francisco. They did not speak Spanish and they had never been to Mexico before. This was their first visit "home." I asked if they were badly hurt and the mother said that her back and buttocks hurt a great deal. She lay in a pile of glass and there was blood around her.

In a few moments the ambulance arrived, World War II vintage. Two stretcher bearers scooped the women up without checking their vital signs or administering any first aid. I looked at Alejandro and he shrugged. "This is Mexico," he said.

I told one of the stretcher bearers that these women were United States citizens and they should be taken to the American-British Hospital and he nodded in agreement. As she was being carried off, the older woman grabbed my hand. "Please, don't leave us," she pleaded with me. Her eyes were filled with terror. "Please. Don't leave us."

I didn't know what to do. The driver of the ambulance said that one person could ride with them. For reasons I still don't understand I handed Alejandro my purse and told him to meet us at the American-British Hospital. He said he'd follow in a taxi. The women, Maria Rivera and her daughter, Estelle, were frightened and in pain. The ambulance had two cots into which the women were strapped, but that was all it had. No cushioned seats, no first-aid equipment of any kind. It was basically just a metal pickup truck with the Red Cross emblem painted on the side.

There were two men in the back of the ambulance and one began to ask me questions. "What is your name and occupation?" I repeated the question, finding it irrelevant, but then I assumed it had something to do with insurance. I told him. Then he asked other questions. The names of the women and their occupations. Did I know them? Were they related? Was I related to them? How had I happened to be at the accident scene? After a while I grew impatient and finally said, "Aren't you going to do something? The woman is in pain." I pointed to the older woman.

"I am just a journalist," he said. "I cover accidents."

"You're the journalist? They send a journalist with the ambulance? So" — I pointed to the man sitting next to him — "is he the paramedic?"

"No, he's the stretcher bearer."

"And the driver?" I asked, feebly, knowing the answer. "He's only the driver."

"You mean there is no paramedic in this ambulance?"

The journalist smiled and wrote down everything I said. I sighed. Mrs. Rivera asked if anything was wrong. I told her nothing was wrong and not to worry. We'd soon be at the American-British Hospital and I would see to it that they got proper care.

In the emergency room a man lay on the floor with a knife sticking out of his thigh. A woman in the throes of labor was writhing on two chairs. Other accident victims were lined up in beds, groaning, some screaming in pain. Blood was everywhere. "Where have you taken us?" I shouted at our driver. "Is this the American-British Hospital?"

He looked at me, bored and indifferent. "They are accident victims. This is the Mexican Red Cross."

The ambulance driver had brought the women to the public hospital, and they were now wards of the state. The daughter, Estelle, understood that something was wrong and became very upset. She had a lot of pain in her neck and shoulder and seemed to be feeling worse, but mainly she knew her mother was bleeding and needed surgery and she recognized that it should not take place here.

For two hours I argued with doctors who wanted to operate on Mrs. Rivera. I told them I had a friend at the American-British Hospital. I told them these women were United States citizens and should be treated at the American-British Hospital. This made them angry, but in truth the reputation of this hospital and of Mexican state hospitals in general was horrendous.

"This woman must have surgery," one of the doctors kept saying. "She is bleeding. She has glass in her rectum."

"Fine, then let me take her to the American hospital."

I argued and argued with them into the night. Mrs. Rivera asked me again and again what was going on and I told her that they wanted to operate on her here. She kept crying, grabbing my hand. "Please, I want to leave this place."

At about three in the morning Alejandro showed, holding my purse. "Thank God you're here," I said, rushing to him.

He had lost the ambulance as we drove through the streets and had gone to the American-British Hospital. When we did not show up there, he decided to try the Mexican Red Cross. Now he stood with us, shaking his head. "This place is awful," he muttered. "We've got to get them out of here."

He went in and talked with the doctors. Through a glass partition, I could see him speaking gently, gesticulating. I watched the doctors nodding, slowly bending to his way.

A half hour later an ambulance was prepared to take all of us to the American-British Hospital. In the ambulance I asked him, "What did you say to them?"

He smiled. "I said Mrs. Rivera's nephew was a surgeon at the American-British Hospital and he was waiting for her. In Mexico," he said, "just mention family. It works every time."

A few moments later we arrived at the emergency room and the Riveras were wheeled into the clean and efficiently run hospital. At about four in the morning, after preliminary examinations, a surgeon, Dr. Eduardo Cruz, was called in. He would operate on Mrs. Rivera. Dr. Cruz was a very gentle, sensitive man with soft brown eyes. "She'll be fine," he told us. "Come back tomorrow."

In the morning the women were doing better, but they did not want to recuperate in Mexico. Arrangements had to be made to transport them back to the United States. A deposit had to be paid on their hospital bill or the hospital would discontinue services. Money needed to be wired. Their things had to be packed, their tours canceled, they had to be checked out of their hotel. And they needed transportation home.

This meant going through an enormous amount of Mexican red tape, but Alejandro was obviously good at that. We liked the Riveras and did what we could. I had enough money to cover the hospital until their money arrived. Alejandro and I took care of the hotel and their belongings. We made the necessary phone calls. We ran all over Mexico

City, changing flights, arranging their departure. It took about four days.

"I don't know what we would have done without you," Mrs. Rivera said. She took down all my addresses, even my parents' in Illinois. "We'll find a way to thank you," they said. "We'll write. We'll let you know how everything is."

I never heard from them again.

5

RETURN

As I approach San Miguel, my ghosts converge. There are two ghosts who go with me most of the time, but there is a new one I feel as I enter my house. One ghost is my maternal grandmother whom I have often felt with me, especially in my room when I am alone at night. She is there like a warm presence and she tries to tell me the things that matter. The other is an unknown ghost whose purpose I do not know, but I believe it is someone from my family who died a sudden and horrible death. At times I think it is the dog my great-uncle Dave buried alive in mud and at other times it is a mysterious lover that one of my aunts was said to have had. This ghost behaves in a different way from my grandmother, who brings comfort and warmth. This stranger always startles me. I wake frightened, heart pounding, and I know I have been visited, but I never know why.

But as I walk up the dusty alleyway late at night, dragging my bags, and open the door of my house, I feel someone is accompanying me. There is a presence in my rooms as I go in; it is no one and nothing I know. But it is not exactly a stranger to me either. This ghost warms my rooms, makes me feel safe.

At various times ghosts or gods run my life. The ghosts I find in my rooms at night, in the eyes of brujas, in the bird nailed to the tree. While the past struggles to keep me back, the gods propel me forward. Into risk and sacrifice, choice and responsibility. The ghosts are in charge of memory; the gods' domain is destiny.

I listen to the ghosts and obey the gods. The ghosts whisper, the gods prod. I listen like a cat at an opening to a wall, and then when it is safe, I pass through. When the gods recede, the ghosts take over and when I let go of the ghosts, some of whom mean me no harm, the gods send me out on my missions. I return to find the infiltration of ghosts.

Sometimes my grandmother herself visits. She sits at the edge of my bed. First she listens to me tell of my grief, then she tells me things I should understand about men. Men, she says, come and go. Men drift in and out. Be yourself, she tells me. Have something that's yours. Of her ninety years, she lived forty-five as a widow and those, she will tell you, were the best. She wanted to be a ballerina and sometimes I can feel her spinning on the floor, trying out a pirouette, my graceful, tiny Russian grandmother.

And sometimes the other ghost visits and I am miserable, for it is a heavy ghost, a ponderous one. Its weight fills the bed. My chest pounds. I gasp for breath. It makes creaking noises intended to frighten me, and they do. It has taken some time to understand that this one will not hurt me, but will frighten me, make me doubt myself. This one makes me think I can't live alone, I can't be alone. This one feels like a jilted lover, someone whose heart has never healed. But I am not the one to love him.

Back in my bed in San Miguel, I feel something else. This new presence. It is like Lupe when I know she is downstairs, even though I haven't spoken with her. But it is not her. I think as I drift to sleep that it must be the woman from the cave in the sierra, the one who bid me welcome, but I have no idea how that could be so.

IN THE MORNING LUPE AND THE CHILDREN WERE waiting for me. They brought fresh flowers and milk for my coffee, warm tortillas, and an avocado, and some eggs. When I opened the door, Lupe said, "At last you are home. We thought you'd be back by now."

Lupe's right arm seemed limp and she held it awkwardly. Also there was a sadness to her face. *"Qué pasa?"* I asked her, jokingly. I had brought gifts for her and for the children and I dug them out of my duffel as I spoke.

She showed me her hand. There was a small puncture wound in her palm and when I squeezed it, puss oozed out. The arm was swollen and her veins protruded. "Lupe," I said, "what have you done?"

"I put my hand down on a nail on that wood of José Luis. It is better now. For two weeks I could not move my arm." I thought how she could get tetanus. The arm looked terrible to me. I told her I'd take her to a doctor in Querétaro. But she shook her head. "It doesn't matter. It is nothing now."

She still seemed sad, so I asked what was wrong.

"I have missed you," she said.

"And that man, José Luis," I asked. "What about him?"

She paused for a moment and then she said, "One of his other señoras, she is having another child." She wiped her eyes with her apron.

"Oh, I am very sorry."

She brushed away my concern. "A man isn't worth crying for." She laughed, but she felt uncomfortable, I could tell, and changed the subject — a trick of hers — to talk about me. "Alejandro, where is he? Will he come to be with you?"

"We are friends. I don't know. I don't want to hurt him."

"He is too serious for you. He doesn't know how to have fun. Mexican men are either too serious and no fun or lighthearted and not to be trusted."

We both laughed at what she said. I made coffee and eggs for all of us. We sat down to eat and a familiar cat with green eyes appeared. I had been gone six weeks and this cat, once skin and bones, now seemed enormous. I told this to Lupe. "The cat looks like a balloon," so we named the cat *Globo*, Spanish for balloon. I realized as I sat in my apartment in San Miguel with Lupe and her children and the cat with the green eyes and Pancha how much I had missed being here. How much I had needed to come home. "I have been away a long time," I said. "I have been on a long trip."

Lupe wiped her eyes once more. "Don't go away again," she said. "Promise me you will stay here."

I shook my head. "Lupe, I can't promise that. I don't know that I can stay here. I don't know how long I'll stay."

"There was a woman," Lupe said, "I worked for her. She was very good to me. After my husband left, I cooked and I did her cleaning. She went home but she said she'd be back in the winter. I never saw her again."

"Well, I won't be that way," I said. I put my hand on hers. "That much I can promise."

That night I am alone. I do not sleep with switchblade or fear, but visions come. The snow falls in thick billows but it is not cold. Soon I am buried beneath it and I can see that it is not really snow. It is the feathers of a great white molting bird. Under the feathers live the gods of the world ånd they discuss how to make the world. They decide to start from scratch. They think of a bird with silver wings whom they will send out to make a survey. They assemble the wings from the feathers beneath which I am hiding. The wings are silent and the bird travels for a long time, returning to show them where to make the world. I enter the dream. I am to be sent to assess the place they have chosen to make the world. To make certain the bird has chosen well. My own arms become wings, great white eagle wings. I set out, pleased with the purpose of my mission.

IT WAS THE SEASON OF THE BULLS AND THOUGH I had never seen or been interested in such a thing, there was a bullfight that Saturday and Derek and Alejandro, who had arrived from Mexico City, wanted to go. I had no desire to go, but both felt it was the kind of thing one should experience while living in Mexico.

We arrived at the bullring in the late afternoon and the stadium was already quite full. The fight would start at four-thirty, but there was music, a band, and much fanfare. Toreadors and picadors walked or rode around the ring, the matadors following, all waving their capes.

There were three matadors — literally, killers — that day: El Queretano (from Querétaro), who seemed to be quite popular, a local hero; Eloy Cavazos, who was the top matador in Mexico; and Curro Rivera, from San Luis Potosí. All three were supposed to be among the finest of Mexico. And then there were the bulls, six of them, who had, I thought, wonderful names. Bonito (beautiful), Azabache (jet black), Insurgente (revolutionary), Pepino (cucumber), Ya Llegé (I have arrived), and Nido de Miel (honeycomb).

Bonito was the first bull to fight and the matador was El Queretano. Bonito came into the ring bewildered and clearly did not want to be there. Instead he seemed to be practicing some form of passive resistance. He ambled around the ring, keeping away from the matador, humiliating him, as if he knew what this game was about and just did not want to play. The picadors came on and thrust long, pointed poles sharply into the bull's back to make him fight, but Bonito still was not very interested. He remained indifferent, walking around the ring, keeping a distance, occasionally making a pass at the frustrated matador.

Finally El Queretano, bored and disgusted, positioned himself and thrust his sword into Bonito's back. Bonito lunged forward, sword not quite deep enough in his shoulder to down him, and caught the matador's cape on the sword. Then the bull dashed around the ring, sword in his back, a cape over his head, as if waving a flag of surrender.

Some of the spectators booed; others laughed. The matador had to find a way to kill the bull. Now the toreadors came out on their padded horses. These men in medieval costume were old — perhaps old matadors — and they seemed to enjoy what they were doing. They jabbed the bull some more. Then Bonito turned on one of the horses, gouging him. The matador, who apparently was in charge of everything, told the picadors and toreadors how much to pick. The picadors kept agitating Bonito, who was finally weakening. El Queretano had another sword and eventually he managed to lunge it firmly into Bonito's shoulder, though by then the bull seemed unconcerned about his fate and grateful for this final thrust.

The actual killing of the bull can take thirty seconds and is fairly painless if it is done properly. A good matador makes the thrust clean into the bull's heart and through his side. But this first fight, everyone around me said, was no fight at all. It was butchery and should have been stopped. Derek was furious. "This is stupid," he kept saying. "Kill the bull," he shouted.

Suddenly Alejandro joined him, with fervor I had never seen in him before. "Kill the bull. Kill the bull." The two men cried together, waving fists in the air. I had to turn away.

The next fight was quick and to the point. The picadors only picked the bull a little and Eloy finished the bull off, after several dramatic, successful passes, with one clean thrust of his sword.

El Queretano was to fight again and I dreaded this, but he had obviously decided to win back the respect he had lost in his first fight. His second bull was Ya Llegé, and El Queretano got down on his knees to greet him. The bull greeted El Queretano by jabbing him in the neck. The picadors began to move in, but El Queretano, not one to suffer further humiliation, ordered them out of the ring. Since Ya Llegé had almost trampled him, this was a very brave thing to do. The crowd went wild and a real fight, such as it was, began.

El Queretano's style was different from Eloy's. Eloy knew exactly how to play each bull and he took no chances. El Queretano — and now I could see why he was a local hero — fought the bull directly until it was exhausted, and then killed it in one swift stroke.

The final fight was as horrible as the first. The matador, Rivera, had the bull picked so badly that blood gushed from an open artery at its neck as if from a whale's spout. Then Rivera killed the bull quickly because it refused to fight. No one applauded; most people had already left the stadium.

Immediately after the fights the bulls are slaughtered for market, and Derek wanted to go out back to see this. Alejandro thought this was a good idea as well. "I've seen enough," I told them.

"Don't you want to see where your beef comes from?" Derek gibed me.

"I'm going home," I said.

Alejandro waved me away. "So go if you like."

I was in bed when Alejandro returned, pounding on the door. Furious with him, I reluctantly went downstairs. "What are you doing?"

"I was having fun." He and Derek had obviously gone drinking.

"You're drunk," I told him. "You're like an Indian when you're drunk."

"I am an Indian," he said, pointing proudly at his chest. "I am an *Azteca*."

"Well, you are an Indian who loves Spanish spectacles," I told him. "Now go to sleep."

In the morning I wanted to hike up to Tres Cruzas, a cliff high above town where three crosses stand, overlooking the whole valley. Alejandro was quite hung over but he agreed to take some aspirin, help me pack a picnic, and go. He actually was familiar with the climb and suggested we visit Three Crosses but then have our picnic in Box Canyon, a place I had never been to. I had heard that during the rainy season a river and waterfall formed there. Even though the season had ended, we had had a great deal of rain; so it seemed possible that we would see the waterfall.

As we set off we were unsure of our route. There was an easy way which was very long, taking us through town, up Happy Valley, past Atascodera, then to Three Crosses. The other way, the "short cut," was to go straight up the mountain directly to Three Crosses. From the base of the valley, the climb did not seem so bad, so I voted for the short cut, never imagining the rocky climb that lay ahead. We set off on a dusty road that soon turned into a scruffy, arid, thorny, cactus-ridden mountainside. We passed two old men sitting by the side of the road and wished them a good afternoon. It was just then noon. The sun was very hot and already I was tired and bringing up the rear. Alejandro was kind enough to slow down for me, and he helped me across the difficult inclines.

But soon I got into the climb. I felt more awake, stronger, less bothered by the heat of the day. I was feeling more vigorous as we came to the place where the real climbing began. Alejandro would climb first, then pull me up. He was carrying almost a full pack, but he seemed agile as we made it through the rough spots. At last we reached a clearing and paused because the view was spectacular. Cactuses bloomed in yellow and pink all around us. Ahead lay the steep mountainside we had just climbed and at the top, still far away, we saw Three Crosses.

We started up again with Alejandro helping me over the steepest inclines. We worked our way slowly, and after a while we took a break and rested on a ridge. Suddenly I jumped and ran forward. I was about to fall a hundred feet when Alejandro reached up and grabbed me. "María," he shouted, "what is wrong?" I pointed to where I'd placed my hand, and what I assumed was a rattlesnake twisted away. Alejandro kicked the snake with his foot and it fell off the ridge. "It is a colebra," he said. "It's not venomous. It won't hurt you."

We reached Three Crosses after about an hour or so of climbing, and we rested with a beer. Then we walked behind Three Crosses, and in the distance I could see the heights of Box Canyon. We made off across the sierra, down a very rocky incline. Alejandro pointed to an anthill and said, "If you let this kind of ant bite your joints, it will cure your arthritis."

I knelt down to look and in doing so put my hand on a cactus. I flinched and pulled away. My hand was full of spines, and I showed it to Alejandro. "Run your hand through your hair," he told me. The electricity, he said, would remove them. I did this, and after a few tries, the spines stopped bothering me.

As we walked on, Alejandro saw a waterspout across the lake in the distance. The Indians, he said, believe that a waterspout is the devil, and they cross themselves and say "Satan, go away" when they see one. Later Alejandro spotted a huge jack rabbit that looked like a kangaroo, dashing behind a cliff.

"You have great eyes," I told him.

"It's in my blood," he said.

When we reached the canyon, at first I was disappointed. Pure rocks, little vegetation. Alejandro suggested we climb down into the canyon to the watering hole for our picnic, so we began our descent of several hundred feet, very rough and rocky, and at last we reached a small oasis — a watering hole at the base of a riverbed surrounded by rocks and trees.

With his Swiss army knife, Alejandro split open a barrel cactus and we sucked on it. It was sweet and not unlike watermelon. Then we laid out our feast. Fried chicken, great egg salad, raw vegetables, nut brownies, a pineapple. We ate ferociously and for a long time. Afterward we stretched out to nap in the sun. Yellow swallowtails hovered overhead and a laughing bird sang from a tree. Behind us was a beautiful green pool of water, and I watched it and dozed.

Then the animals came. Hundreds of them. They came from all the sides of the canyon. Goats and sheep and horses and donkeys. One horse climbed down the canyon with his front feet tied together. I don't know how he made it down. Behind the animals came the shepherds and some young boys with machetes, who begged from us the rest of our food; we gave it to them and to the shepherds. Soon the canyon was filled with leaping goats and sheep, donkeys braying and kicking high.

I decided I wanted to bring back a little kid as a present for Lisa, and I found one I wanted — a tiny black goat with big blue eyes. I bartered with the shepherd over it. He wanted one hundred fifty pesos, but we had only eighty. I picked up the little goat and it lay in my lap like a baby, and I tried to convince the shepherd to sell it to me, but he would not budge from his high price.

Suddenly, as quickly as they'd come, the animals went away. They leaped up and scaled the canyon walls. I was very surprised, but Alejandro told me that each group of animals has its leader, and they know when to leave by following their leader. He said we should probably leave as well. It was almost four o'clock and we had a long walk back.

We packed up and walked slowly now. A falcon circled overhead. Poor people came to their doorways and waved as we passed their houses. We reached the center of town at six o'clock and paused for a much needed soft drink. When I got home all the children were waiting and they were very excited.

At about four o'clock that afternoon a small goat had come to their door. After telling me this, they ran off and produced a black kid, blue-eyed, just like the one I had wanted to buy for Lisa. The next day, when its owner came to find it, I paid him a few dollars and Lisa kept the goat.

That night we made a fire and cooked a big pot of vegetable soup with chicken and avocado. Lupe and the children joined us. Afterward Alejandro and I sat, reading peacefully, in front of the fire. It was one of those perfect moments, one of those rare times life affords us, and I wanted to take it away clear and pure.

We closed our books at about midnight and were about to go to bed when someone pounded on the door. "Alejandro, I know you are there. You scum, you slime." Alejandro looked at me, forlorn. "Go upstairs," he told me.

He opened the door and I heard more shouting. It was Carlos, his Spaniard friend. "Fuck your slut of a mother," Carlos said over and over again. At last Alejandro came upstairs. "Can Carlos sleep downstairs? He is drunk and I had promised him that I would do some business with him on Friday and I forgot. He drove all the way from Mexico City, drunk, to tell me off."

"If he made it this far, why can't he go to his mother's?" She lived in Guanajuato, about an hour away.

"She'll be furious to find him like this."

We brought Carlos in, but he was drunk and abusive to both of us. When we finally got upstairs, Alejandro said, "I'm sorry. This ruined our day."

"Yes," I said. "You could say it did."

"I'll find a way to make it up to you," he told me.

"Just don't let it happen again," I said.

Alejandro left with Carlos in the morning, saying he'd return in a week or two, and I was glad to see him go. I settled back into solitude. I worked in the morning when I could. José Luis was in the process of building a house nearby and he had a work crew in Lupe's yard, hammering all day long. Some days when the noise was too much for me, I went with them to the work site. They were building a colonial house for a rather wealthy family from Mexico City. The house had a patio and ceramic tiles.

I'd sit on the ground near the house and watch as the men put up beams and mixed cement. Lupe was in charge of carting huge bags of the cement mix from the pickup truck to the men. She'd hoist a fifty-pound sack on her back and carry it as if it were a child riding piggyback. One day she stopped and put the bag down in front of me. "Here, María," she said. "You carry one." When I could not even budge it, she laughed hysterically and so did all the men.

One morning a man knocked at my door. He was selling strawberries. I told him I would buy a box and went upstairs to get some money. When I returned, he was in the kitchen, going through the drawers. He looked at me, ashamed, and said he was looking for a knife to clean the strawberries with. He wanted to rob me, I knew, but I said nothing. I bought another box from him instead.

In the mornings I watched all the children of San Antonio heading off to school. They went in hordes in red and white uniforms. One day I said to Lupe, "Isn't it time for Lisa and Agustín to go?"

"They need uniforms," Lupe said. "They can't go to school without them."

"Are uniforms expensive?"

She told me the cost of the uniforms, which wasn't very much. "Well, shall we buy them uniforms? Do you want them to go to school?"

"I don't want them to grow up to be a burro like me."

So we bought the uniforms and made the necessary arrangements for the younger children to attend school.

In the afternoons, I climbed into the hills. No matter how long I'd been away or how far I'd gone, something always drew me back to San Miguel and to those hills. I could not really pinpoint it. But when I left Mexico City it was to get back here. To the place I was beginning to think of as home.

In my life I have known every joy and every sorrow and each has been short-lived. I have known what I thought to be great love and tremendous loss. I have wandered in the labyrinth of myself and thought that somehow I was living life intensely, with deep feeling. Now I know differently. I was a victim of the forces outside myself, and more than that, I was victim to my ego. I knew it was the ego that blocked the soul. Joy and despair were mere reflections of how well I fared in the world.

But in San Miguel, with Lupe and the children and the animals, I found something else, and it was not so short-lived. When the children came to my door, when the tortilla lady or the flower lady or the avocado man or whoever came to my door, or when I was simply alone, on the roof, staring for hours, daydreaming, doing nothing at all, I felt a kind of peace come over me. I have felt this elsewhere — in Tibet and Machu Picchu — but those were special places, holy places. This was just a dusty old place, but for me it had become everything. I was simply enjoying the experience of being, of living without goal or expectation, without longing or desire. I was happy when I was there — happy just to be.

Sometimes I'd see the woman who came out of her cave and stood at the edge of the hills. I had seen her a few times now and it was beginning to occur to me that each time I saw her, she was younger and more beautiful, her hair more silken, her face less wrinkled. I wondered how young she would become before it was my time to leave. I wanted to get closer to her, but as I approached she disappeared back into the cave, though I could not be sure. The one thing I was sure of was that when I was near this woman, I felt her presence and it felt the same to me as whatever it was that had been warming my rooms.

I wanted to touch her. I wanted to know her. And as I walked the sierra in the afternoons, the odd thought came to me — that to know her I had to know myself. And another thought came. That somehow I already did know her. I just had not yet made the connection as to how.

One evening when I got back to my house, Lupe was

sweeping out front. "Sometimes when I go into the sierra, I see a woman. She seems to be watching me. Do you know who she is?"

Lupe looked at me and laughed. "Some say it is my mother." Then she shrugged and returned to her sweeping. "But she's dead, so I know that can't be."

Lupe's hand and arm didn't seem to be getting better and she wasn't feeling well. She had a friend in Querétaro she wanted to visit and thought she'd see a doctor as well. I told her I'd go with her and help with the children, and at the end of the week we went.

Lupe didn't look well as we boarded the bus. Lisa and Pollo and one of Lupe's older daughters, Teresa, were with us — the girls all dressed up for their venture to Querétaro. On the bus Pollo sat on my lap, face pressed to the glass. She had never taken this road before. She had never left her safe San Miguel home.

When we reached Querétaro, Lupe led us to the doctor. I took the children to a playground nearby and we stayed for an hour or so. We returned just as Lupe was leaving the doctor's office. He patted her on the back. "Take care of yourself." He looked with dismay at the children. "And get some rest."

"How is her arm?" I asked.

"Her arm?" the doctor said. "She didn't say anything about her arm."

Lupe looked at me sheepishly, then showed the doctor her hand. He looked at it and said, "It is better now. You should have had a tetanus shot, but now it is all right."

We left the clinic and I didn't say anything to her for a while. "So, what did you see the doctor about?" I finally asked. "You don't have to tell me if you don't want to."

"It pains me to tell you, Mary." She spoke in a low voice. We were walking somewhere. Lupe seemed to know where, so I followed. I knew before she spoke that she was pregnant. I don't know why I hadn't noticed; María Elena, her eldest

[140]

daughter, was pregnant too, and I had been one of the first to comment on her enlarged figure and growing despondence. I shook my head. "How are you going to manage?"

She shrugged. "I've managed so far."

We were walking to her friend's house. We walked for almost an hour in the heat and dust of Querétaro. We walked into a very poor neighborhood, but here at least there were houses, not like in the poorer sections of San Antonio where people live in shacks. At last we stopped at one of the houses and Lupe knocked. After a few moments some children rushed out. They called for their mother. Then their mother rushed out. She was very glad to see Lupe. She was an older woman, perhaps in her late forties, and Lupe told me she had ten children.

"Please," she said, "come in." We entered a long vestibule filled with plants and caged birds. The birds were dingy and sick-looking and the plants withering, but it was nicer than many Mexican homes I had been to. Surrounded by her children, we followed her into the living room.

On the couch lay one of her daughters, a girl of about nineteen. She wore a white nightgown and she snored in the deepest, most guttural snore I have ever heard. Her mouth was open and she did not move as we sat down. The señora, who seemed cheerful, asked one of her children to bring us tea. She seated herself beside the daughter on the couch, pushed her over slightly, patted her gently. I expected the girl to get up and leave. Instead she snored more deeply, her breathing shaking the room.

"And so," the woman said, "how have you been? And all the children?" This woman had lived in San Miguel and knew Lupe from there. Finally Lupe asked about the girl on the couch and the señora said, almost nonchalantly, that the girl had been this way for five days. "She took some drugs. She is in a coma."

I couldn't believe we were having tea with a girl in a coma. We sat and talked about children, about life in San Miguel. After an hour or so, with the girl in the coma still snoring, motionless, we said good-bye and walked back to the bus station to return to San Miguel. Later we learned that the girl was dying. A doctor had come to look at her and had said nothing could be done, so they had left her there on the sofa.

I had an odd dream that night that has proved to be prophetic. A cat is being carried off by black mice. The cat has lived a long time and has had thirty years of suffering. Her wounds are purple. When I find her, she offers no resistance. I remember thinking to myself as I am dreaming this dream, a cat would fight off the mice; the mice would not attack the cat. But in this dream the situation is reversed. I tend to the cat. Her insides fall out like filleted steaks. A man I know but cannot name comes and wipes these innards clean. He washes each organ in water. The cat doesn't die but stares at her insides. Somehow she will live.

6

THE HIGHLANDS

I STOOD AT TALISMAN BRIDGE IN A FRONTIER TOWN called El Carmen, awaiting the bus to Quezalte-nango. Guatemala was in front of me, Mexico was behind, and I hoped the name Talisman would mean some kind of good luck for me. Huge orange and yellow butterflies flew as the Zuchiate Río rapids rushed by. A woman with a basket of fruit on her head offered to sell me a strange red fruit I'd never seen before.

After a terrible evening the previous night in a lifeless room in Tapachula, a border town, I was about to enter Guatemala. My plan was to travel through Guatemala either to the ruins of Copán or into Salvador, as far south as I could go, depending on the time. I wanted to be back in Mexico within a few weeks.

A line in the guidebook caught my eye. "Warning: As political instability in the country increases, it is advisable not to stray too far from the beaten track." It was not my intention to stray that far, but the whole journey was probably unsafe. I would not go as far north as Huehuete-nango, where the worst would occur, but there had already been problems near my destination. I had heard that a priest had been killed in a small village on the far side of Lake Atitlán, across from Panajachel, where I was headed. Friends in Mexico City had told me not to go, but I wanted to see Guatemala for myself, and so I went.

I had come to the land of the resplendent quetzal, that elusive and magnificent bird deemed by some to be the most remarkable bird in the world — a bird of such beauty and mystery that the conquistadors thought it a mythical crea-ture, a bird born in the imagination of the Guatemala Maya. Indeed the image of the great god Quetzalcóatl, the plumed serpent, is that of a flying quetzal. But though endangered, the quetzal was and is very real. The ancient Maya considered the blue-green iridescent tail feathers of the male to be better than gold. They traded these feathers throughout Mesoamerica, and today the dollar equivalent in Guatemala is called a quetzal. But the real value of the quetzal bird is intangible. Its specialness is not unlike the specialness of the indigenous peoples whom it represents.

In 1542 Cortés dispatched Pedro de Alvarado, the conquistador who had slaughtered the Aztecs while they were performing a religious ceremony, to Guatemala. Alvarado proceeded to torture, rape, and kill as many indigenous people as he was able. Bartolomé de Las Casas reported how Alvarado forced Indians to eat the flesh of their dead and killed children, broiling them for eating. According to Las Casas, Alvarado was responsible for some five million deaths — probably an exaggeration, but nonetheless it gives a sense of the extent of the conquest.

In *The Tears of the Indians* Las Casas wrote of Alvarado, "How many orphans did he make, how many families did he rob of their sons, how many husbands did he deprive of their wives, how many women did he leave without husbands, how many married women did he adulterate, how many virgins did he ravish, how many did he enslave."

While I awaited the bus through the highlands, a truck arrived. Women stood by with sacks and pitchers while men began unloading containers of flour and cooking oil, stamped FROM THE PEOPLE OF THE UNITED STATES OF AMERICA in English, Chinese, Japanese, Hebrew, Spanish, and many other languages. I was merely a tourist, but I was also a gringa, a North American, and the deeper I would travel into Central America, the more aware I would become of who I was and of how people identified me with my country. And I would become more aware of my country's role in that region. The irony of these women receiving flour from the United States was not lost on me.

At the height of the Cold War in the 1950s, United States

foreign policy in Central America because interventionist again, as it had in early parts of our history. In 1954 the CIA brought about the overthrow of the democratically elected Guatemalan president, Arbenz, whose platform stood for an end of corrupt rule and a distancing from North American influence. A military dictatorship was then established with the goal of infantilizing and virtually enslaving the indigenous peoples of the northern highlands of Guatemala. These people, however, rebelled. They formed small bands that roamed the hills. They established a guerrilla movement much as they had when Pedro de Alvarado was dispatched by Cortés to conquer these highlands.

The government would soon make war on its civilian population — a population that had grown accustomed to being made war upon, and to fighting back. Like the quetzal which is their symbol, the Mayan people were endangered. I was traveling in a lull before the storm.

The bus arrived and we drove through the highlands. The landscape was astounding. It was how I pictured ancient China. Gentle rolling hills terraced in evenly spaced rows where corn and beans grew. In some cases every inch of a hill was terraced, not unlike the terracing of a Mayan pyramid, but here it was a whole hillside, a mountain. Farmers worked in the hills. Women in elaborately woven blouses and skirts carried huge baskets of grain on their heads and waved as the bus drove by. Others bent into streams, scrubbing clothing against rocks or letting down their long black hair to wash it in the cool mountain streams.

Coming out of a rain shower into the sun, we passed the mountainside village of Zunil. The houses were made of a white clay and the roofs were red tile. The village reminded me of the illustrations in books I'd read as a child — those perfect little villages where everything is peaceful — and I longed to stop. From the road I could see fires burning. I imagined children playing, happy families. I have always tried to picture the life within houses. I especially like to do this at night when I can see a light burning in a bedroom, the blue glow of a TV from a living room, candlelight on the dining room table. Perhaps I long to live in other people's houses, other people's lives. But seeing the village of Zunil, I longed for home.

If I'd been in a car, I would have stopped, but I had no idea when the next bus would come by. In my mind I attributed not stopping to logistics. I wanted to reach Quezaltenango by evening and Panajachel the next day. But I must admit I was afraid. The line in the guidebook had done its trick. I would not stray far. Looking back, I'm not sure I would have stopped no matter what, and I'm glad I didn't, for Zunil remains fixed in my memory as a perfect place, a perfect village, a place of perfect peace. If I had stopped, probably I would have found something else.

That evening I wandered the cobbled streets of Quezal-tenango — a modern city, but with narrow colonial-looking streets and low adobe and tile-roofed houses. But it was cold and rainy and I had no desire to be outside. Instead I returned early to the dreary room with no windows I had taken in a run-down boarding house. There I fell asleep at seven o'clock, feeling miserable and alone.

In the morning I got the bus to Panajachel. A friend in Mexico had written to a friend of hers named Eleanore McCauley, who lived in Panajachel in the house where Che Guevara had once lived, asking if I could stay with her. I knew little about Eleanore except that she was a Bostonian who'd moved to Guatemala to try to help the Indians with their production of high-protein products.

We reached Panajachel in the afternoon, and I went with a little map in hand through the muddy streets to find Eleanore McCauley's house. The house was supposed to be across the street from a restaurant, the Pájaro Azul (blue bird), and a horrible discotheque, but it took some stomping through the mud to find it. At last I located the Pájaro Azul and across from it the house where Che Guevara had lived. Pinned to the door was a weathered and rain-streaked note that had obviously been there for many days. It read, "Mary Morris, had to go to U.S.A. Find Patricia." And again a little map.

The map was very simple and I followed it around the corner to a lovely pagoda-like house surrounded by birds of paradise and assorted tropical flowers. I saw a toucan with a limp wing sitting on a perch but no sign of Patricia. Two other structures were sketched on the map, representing a small guest house and then, a few more yards back, another house on the property. I continued through this paradisiacal setting and knocked on the door of the house.

A man came out who looked remarkably like my uncle Sidney. "Are you Mary Morris?" he asked. He introduced himself as Walter Weinstein and said he'd been waiting for me. "Eleanore said you'd make it here eventually. She had to go to the States for some legal matters and asked Patricia and me to help you out." He explained to me that Patricia was his landlady. "We expected you last week." He got a rather wistful look in his eye and I could tell he'd been looking forward to my company. "Anyway, the guest house is yours." He pointed in the direction of the small cottage with high windows shielded by a grove of fruit trees, thick with plantains and lemons.

We sat down on his porch and Walter brought out a tray of fresh fruit juices — mango and orange and papaya — and small cakes. I stretched out in a bamboo chair and sipped the nectar that Walter said his gardener had squeezed that morning. "So," Walter asked, "where are you from?" I told him I was from New York and he said he was from Illinois.

"Oh," I said, "I'm originally from Illinois."

"What part?"

"The North Shore."

He nodded. "I'm from the North Shore."

"I'm from Highland Park," I said.

"So am I," Walter replied. "You aren't related to the

Morrises from Highland Park, are you? Sidney and Ruth?"

"As a matter of fact, you look like my uncle Sidney," I said.

"Everybody used to say that," Walter replied. "Your parents aren't Rosalie and Sol, are they?"

"Why, yes, they are," I replied, thinking this was getting very strange indeed.

"And you went to the Ravinia Nursery School, right?"

"Right," I said, dumbfounded.

It turned out that Walter Weinstein and his wife, Janine, were friends of my aunt and uncle and knew my parents. Janine had been my teacher at the Ravinia Nursery School a quarter of a century before.

We settled into an afternoon of cocktails and reminiscences about home. Walter told me about himself. He had retired from a nondescript civil service job he hadn't liked and had decided he wanted to live his life differently. He wanted to get away from America and from the bourgeois life, and so he'd given up everything to move to Panajachel. Including Janine. Janine had come down and given it a try, but she'd been unhappy. Walter seemed to be still in love with her and was hoping to work it out.

"My life is good here," he said, nursing a piña colada. "I've got this house that I rent from Patricia. I've got a little boat I sail. The natives are nice to me. I can't complain."

We had talked for a few hours when Walter said he'd make dinner. I decided to go for a walk down by the lake. I had not really seen the lake when I arrived and I wanted to visit the town a little before dark. I told Walter I was going, put my pack inside the Japanese-style guest house, and walked the half mile to the lake.

Lake Atitlán is famous for its changing hues, the way the light moves across its surface, from shades of aquamarine to fuchsia, from cobalt blue to scarlet. I walked down toward the water through this small town of muddy streets, indigenous peoples, and foreigners such as Walter Weinstein.

Women passed, their hair wrapped in colored beads made from polished stones found along the lake's shores, beads that were the same colors as the light reflected on the lake, which glistened in the setting sun. They wore bright red and green shawls across their shoulders, with infants wrapped inside. The men of Panajachel wore plainer clothes, white shirts and dark trousers. This has been the case in Central America since at least 1932, when El Salvador's General Maximiliano Hernandez Martínez ordered the massacre of all males in native costumes. About thirty thousand people died in this event, called simply *la Matanza*, the massacre. In recent years in Guatemala, with the renewed slaughter, women have also adopted Western dress as a means of survival.

A group of women, accompanied by young girls, also in bright dresses and shawls, stopped me. The women held up long strands of beads and tried to sell them to me. I paused and for a few moments we bargained, not seriously, though. They dangled the beads and draped them over my head. I laughed and said they had to make me a better price. They said that tomorrow they would make me a better price. Spanish was a foreign language to these women. Their native tongue was Quiché, and some of them spoke English, French, or German as well as they spoke Spanish. They were good traders, but with me, at that moment, they were mainly having fun.

I asked where they came from. Pointing up the hill, they told me they were returning to their village just above Panajachel, called Sololá. The following year I would read in the newspapers how the people of Sololá had been killed in terrible ways. The lucky ones had fled to Mexico and are probably still living in refugee camps.

Patricia arrived later that evening with the crippled toucan, whom she introduced as Calamity, sitting on her arm. An enormous silver dog named Toscanini, with one blue eye and one gray, followed her. "We were expecting you." Patricia smiled at the toucan and patted the dog. "We knew you were coming soon," she said rather mysteriously.

Patricia was a woman touched by some spirit. She was a

large Nordic-looking woman who loved animals and was usually followed by a cat or a dog or had a bird perched on her arm. Calamity, she explained, had been found in the jungle. Some feather traders had tried to capture her and had broken her wing. An Indian brought her to Patricia, who adopted Calamity and made her well. Patricia was known as the St. Francis of Panajachel. But to me she was a somewhat distant woman with a cold streak. I never quite made contact with her, though I tried.

As we sat down to dinner, Patricia volunteered that she believed in the teachings of Sai Baba. She said that in front of her very eyes he had produced from thin air a golden locket with a picture of Shiva on it. Behind her, Walter winked.

Walter had made a kind of stew with rice and beans, which was quite good. "Have you been here a long time?" I asked Patricia.

"Twenty-five years," she told me.

"That's a lifetime," Walter said. He had been there four years and now he told me he was thinking of going back to the States. "There's trouble here," he said. He repeated what I'd already heard. That a priest had been killed across the lake and that there'd been killings near Huehuetenango. "People predict that all the indigenous are in for trouble."

"A lot of Americans are getting ready to get out," Patricia said, looking toward the highlands, distracted. "But I'll stay."

"You will stay? No matter what happens?"

Patricia moved her hand in front of her face as if brushing cobwebs away. "I've seen God come out of thin air. I believe whatever happens is meant to happen."

Tell that to someone in prison, I wanted to say; tell that to someone being tortured. But I was a guest and Patricia was not of this world. Walter could see I was getting annoyed with her and he switched the subject. "What are your plans?" he asked me. My only plan was to cover as much ground as possible. I wanted to travel as far as I could through Central America and then fly back from whatever country I'd made it to. Walter asked me where I thought that would be.

"Either Salvador or Honduras," I said.

"Well, if you go anywhere," Walter said — and he was already sounding a bit dubious about my venture — "I'd go to Honduras. There's trouble there, but there's trouble everywhere else and a lot more of it."

"Yes." Patricia nodded, now struck by the reality of the journey I was making. "I'd go to Honduras if I were you."

On Sunday I set off to the market in Chichicastenango. Walter said that the market was just for tourists and I should spend a relaxing day by the lake, but I had heard about it for so long and so I had to go. The packed bus left Panajachel at about eight and by ten we had arrived.

Chichicastenango is the hub of the Quiché Maya highlands. In the town itself about one thousand *ladinos*, or Spanish descendants, live. But in the hills around the town some twenty thousand Maya dwell, and on market days they come into the town to sell their wares. Outside of the church and market, Chichicastenango is nondescript — low rain-damaged dirt-floor houses; small shops that sell gum, candles, and Fanta; and cantinas.

I wandered through the market where mostly women, often with children clinging to their breasts, shawls wrapped around them, sold small coin purses, sweaters, embroidered ponchos, skirts, *huipiles* (embroidered blouses). They bartered in broken French, English, German, and Spanish, and giggled among themselves in their own tongue.

I paused to buy a purse from a woman. She wore beads in her hair and the traditional skirt. But instead of a huipil she wore a Donald Duck T-shirt. I stared at the T-shirt in disbelief. "Where did you get that?"

She displayed it for me proudly. A North American, she told me, wanted to buy her huipil and he gave her five dollars plus this T-shirt in exchange. I asked if this was common practice and she said yes. "Many North Americans want our blouses. So we trade them for the blouses they bring."

I wandered over to see the Dominican monastery and the famous St. Tomas Church. The monastery was the place where in 1690 the manuscript of the *Popol Vuh*, the book of Quiché Maya mythology, was discovered, and where Father Jiménez worked on its translation. It is one of the few books left to us, since many Mayan mythologies were destroyed in Bishop Diego de Landa's infamous book burning in 1562, in which many of the secrets of Mayan beliefs and culture were destroyed because they were considered heretical. The mysteries of these people have been lost, and what little remains comes to us through the *Popol Vuh*.

At St. Tomas the ceremony was under way. On the steps of the church, Maya knelt, incanting in their own tongue and burning copal candles, flower petals, and a thick incense. Inside, Mass was in process. The Maya of Chichicastenango hold firmly to their pagan beliefs. A number of years ago they made an arrangement with an ingenious priest. The Indians could pray to their own gods on the steps of the church. Then they would go inside and pray to the Christian god.

I could not help but think, here in this ancient village, confronted with indigenous women in Donald Duck T-shirts and men on the steps of churches, praying to pagan gods, what reality had been for these people for the past four hundred years. In these highlands, which have been called both *Tierra de la Guerra* (land of war) and *Verdadera Paz* (true peace), their struggle has been long and intense.

7

AT THE BORDER

ON THE ROAD TO GUATEMALA CITY I HAD TO change buses at Chimultenango. I got off the bus. A man was urinating into a ditch by the side of the road. An old woman, descending from the bus, recognized the man. "Hola, Pepito," she said to him. The man, recognizing her as well, waved back with a smile, his urine streaming into the gully.

I waited at the side of the road, by some small stands where tacos, Chiclets, and warm Fanta were sold. A boy slept on the embankment. Three policemen came by. They kicked him, poked him with their sticks. They kicked him harder and he woke screaming, pleading for mercy, as they dragged him off. Everyone looked away.

A girl of about sixteen with a baby wrapped in a shawl on her back had a small stand of candy, cigarettes, and cigars. She wore native clothing and smoked one of her cigars. "Is it a good cigar?" I asked her, surprised to see a girl smoking one.

She explained to me that it was a cigar girls smoked to bring on images of their future husbands. "Are you married?" she asked. I told her I was not. "Then you must try one." She laughed, handing me a cigar.

I told her no, thank you, I wasn't interested in such images. I walked on, but still the bus didn't come. I walked back again and said I'd try. "Here." She gave it to me for a few cents. She held a lighter and I lit it. I took a puff but nothing happened. "So?" she asked.

"*Nada,*" I replied.

"Try again."

I did. This time an image came. I saw someone tall with soft brown eyes, older and bald. A nice smile, benevolent eyes. The image sharpened. There were books and papers. A studious man. Then I saw tennis rackets, boxer shorts. Piles of dishes and a Sunday afternoon football game.

I told her what I'd seen. "Nobody's perfect," she said, laughing as if she knew of what she spoke.

The bus terminal in Guatemala City looks like a traveler's vision of hell — thousands of dilapidated, idling buses facing in every direction, sitting in clouds of fumes. There were buses to Managua, to San Salvador, buses to Mexico City, buses to Laredo and to Panama City. I wanted to go to Salvador but the man who was selling tickets looked at me dubiously. "I won't sell you a ticket to Salvador," he told me. "The border is bad," he said. "It's not safe for you to go that way alone. Why don't you go to Copán." I was inexperienced with bus travel in Central America but decided that the ticket seller probably knew what he was talking about. I bought a ticket to Copán, the Mayan ruins at the border with Honduras.

I had time to kill so I walked around near the bus terminal. Not far from the bus terminal was a garbage dump. As trucks pulled into the dump, dropping their loads, the dump became a swarm of life. Small children picked through the rubble, coming up with a chicken bone or a scrap of lard. They rushed off, kicking diseased dogs who tried to take the bones from them. Women grabbed for bits of cloth, old men scavenged for scraps of wood or tin. Everyone dug for food, for whatever they could find. Some stuffed it in their mouths right there. Others hid it in their pockets. A boy I'd seen running with food from the dump came up to me, begging. I asked him about the dump. "Are you always here?"

"Oh, no," he said. "It's just that at this hour the trucks come in from where the rich people live and from the hotels. The food is very good right now."

I found a telegraph office and cabled Alejandro to say I'd be home the following Friday. Then I left the highlands behind and took the bus toward Copán. The landscape changed immediately. The terrain turned rough and tropical, the poverty even more severe, the people no longer Indian but *mestizo*, mixed blood, and they looked different from those in the highlands. These people of the hot, tropical lowlands seemed tired and spent, without hope, impoverished. Already I missed Panajachel and the magical elegance of the highlands.

Everything changed. There were road checks along the way. Police stopped our bus at random, waved it over. They boarded with submachine guns and demanded identity cards. A woman behind me whispered that this was to stop tax evaders and illegals, but it looked like something else to me. You don't need to stop tax evaders with submachine guns. The women put their heads down. The men looked away. Some of the men were taken off the bus and the bus drove away. One of the women wailed.

We drove on. The bus got a flat tire and we were delayed an hour while the tire was changed. I was nervous that I wouldn't reach Copán by evening and would have to find a place to stay along the way. I wasn't exactly on the tourist trail now and everything felt different. What had been hinted at in the highlands was out in the open here. We reached another checkpoint, soldiers and army this time. Soldiers wearing T-shirts, rifles at their sides, lay under a palapa. People were ordered off the bus. The bus drove on and the passengers acted as if nothing had happened. The woman who was wailing before had stopped; I glanced at her and she stared ahead, blank and dumbstruck.

The bus went on and I approached the driver. "Copán, right?" I asked, and he nodded. "Copán," he said. But I had no idea where we were. The names of the towns didn't correspond to anything on my map. We reached a river and a downed bridge at the crest of a waterfall. The bus driver just drove across this waterfall. I peered down the drop of the falls. On the other side the water rushed. I thought of the boy at Agua Azul and watched as he went over the falls again and again.

At a place called Chiquimula I was told I must change buses. While I waited for the bus to take me the rest of the way, I was attacked by a woman with no teeth. She chased me around a pile of coconuts. Some men tried to help, but the woman kept chasing me. Finally, still grabbing at me, the woman collapsed on the ground. She lifted up her skirt and spread her legs while all the men, mostly bus drivers, stood around laughing.

At about three o'clock I boarded a minibus for Copán. I was glad to get out of Chiquimula, to ride through the mountainous tropical jungle of southern Guatemala, until at about six o'clock the bus stopped. The driver motioned for me. "Jocotán," he said. "Copán," I replied, but he shook his head, indicating I was to get off here. "Jocotán," he said. I had never heard of Jocotán, but from what I could see from the window, I was fairly certain I didn't want to be there.

But the bus driver made it clear that this was the end of the line for me that day. As I got off, he explained that I had to spend the night here. "At five A.M. a truck will come and take you to Copán," he said, and then he drove away.

I stood in the middle of a dusty square, boiling and tropical, amidst skinny dogs with open sores, chickens with tumors all over them, hordes of flies, enormous flowers I had never seen before. A steady drumbeat in the distance would continue into the night.

I managed to find one of the only pensions in town, the Pensión Ramirez. A very nice old mestizo woman with gray hair showed me a room. It consisted of bamboo walls without windows, a straw mattress on a dirt floor. Because I do the best I can to protect myself, I am not usually concerned about rare tropical diseases. But there is one disease, called Chagas disease, which terrifies me, and it can be acquired on dirt floors frequented by opossums. The opossums carry an insect called an assassin bug which bites you and then defecates in the wound. The feces enter your blood system and the parasite incubates there for one to twenty years. The first symptoms resemble those of malaria, but in the end it behaves more like AIDS.

I did not know if the disease occurred in that part of the continent and I didn't know the word for opossum, so I tried to describe the animal to the woman. She looked at me quizzically. Then, thinking I was displeased with her facilities, she grew concerned. "No, no rats," she swore up and down. "No rats."

For a dollar and one night I decided I'd be all right. From the porch I could see the mountains and the jungle where I would go the next day. I took an ice-cold shower in a kind of open outdoor hut. Standing wet and naked at the edge of the jungle, with thatched roofs in the distance, I was glad to be off that bus and about to cross into another country. Giant bees buzzed around and I noticed again that the flowers were very, very big.

I headed back to the center of Jocotán to try to find a place to eat. As I walked, I heard someone call my name. "Mary," a voice said. "Is that you?" To my surprise, there stood Jean-Paul, a Belgian whom I'd met at a café in Mexico City a few months before. Jean-Paul had indicated then that he wanted to see me again, and I think he was nonplused for it to be at the border at Jocotán, while traveling with his maladjusted son and his very fat wife, who had a staple in her ear. But he seemed very happy, almost desperate, to see me. They were coming from Copán and assured me that in fact Jocotán was a sort of dropping-off point for people on their way to the ruins. Clearly tourism had not hit Jocotán, yet I was relieved to know a truck would pick me up and take me to the border.

Jean-Paul's wife, Françoise, was an art historian and very nice, though she kept touching the staple, which she said suppressed her desire to eat. But all she could think about was eating, and she suggested I join them for dinner. They had already planned to dine with someone from their pension, so we all headed off in the direction of the main square.

Josh Greenbaum was an economist from Berkeley who

was traveling through Central America; he had come from Tikal via Belize. Josh told me this in the few moments it took to walk from the main square to the "restaurant" we found, which consisted of two tables in somebody's backyard. We swatted flies and drank beer, awaiting the *especialidad de la casa* — a dish called *ropa vieja* (old clothes).

"How long have you been traveling?" I asked Josh.

"Oh, only four weeks this time. I have to be back in Berkeley in two weeks."

"You're traveling alone?"

He nodded. He had silky brown hair that fell across his brow and wonderful cocoa-brown eyes. "And you?"

"Yes," I said.

"My God," Françoise piped in, rubbing her staple. "I could never do such a thing. Aren't you nervous? Aren't you afraid? I couldn't stand it. I absolutely would find it intolerable."

"I meet people along the way," I said.

Josh asked me where I was going. "To Copán," I said. "Then back to Mexico City via Tegucigalpa. And you?" I asked him.

"Oh, I'm not sure. Maybe to Panama. Probably to Guatemala City. Maybe straight to San Jose. I've never seen Copán."

"Well, I leave crack of dawn."

He shook his head. "I'm going west."

"Well, Josh" — Françoise was back in the conversation — "you shouldn't let her go alone. Why don't you go to Copán?"

He shrugged. "I've seen enough ruins," he replied.

We dropped the subject of travel and had a fairly pleasant dinner of ropa vieja — a kind of shredded beef — and rice. Jean-Paul and Françoise said they were on their way back to Belgium from a year in Mexico City, and Emmanuel, who had some fairly serious socialization problems, seemed thrilled to be getting out of Latin America. He had acne and several nervous ticks. As he complained about being dragged around in the tropical heat, his face twitched in unspeakable ways.

After dinner we sat in the main square and a procession passed. It must have been a religious celebration, but it was very weird. Christ in armor, sword in hand, rode on horseback, looking distinctly like Cortés. Firecrackers popped and men who marched behind him beat a single, steady beat on lone drums. Lobotomized-looking people, expressionless, dead faces, followed. The procession left me with the sense that anything could happen here.

Josh walked me back to my pension. We strolled slowly in the heat of the evening. "Well, it was very nice meeting you," he said as we reached the pension.

"It was nice," I said.

"Have a safe journey." He kissed me on the cheek. I wished him a safe journey as well.

Returning to the pension, I climbed into a hammock outside, at the edge of the jungle, waiting for the heat to drop, listening to the sounds of the night. I found myself completely absorbed by a chirp, a hoot, a cry, a bark, a call, a whisper, a shriek.

I have no idea how long I stayed in the hammock, listening to the birds and distant monkeys and that steady beat of a drum, almost tribal, which resonated through the night. But it was a long time before I got up and wandered into my room to sleep on the ground in a bed of straw.

WOMEN WHO TRAVEL AS I TRAVEL ARE DREAMERS. Our lives seem to be lives of endless possibility. Like readers of romances we think that anything can happen to us at any time. We forget that this is not our real life — our life of domestic details, work pressures, attempts and failures at human relations. We keep moving. From anecdote to anecdote, from hope to hope. Around the next bend something new will befall us. Nostalgia has no place for the woman traveling alone. Our motion is forward, whether by train or daydream. Our sights are on the horizon, across strange terrain, vast desert, unfordable rivers, impenetrable ice peaks.

I wanted to keep going forever, to never stop, that morning when the truck picked me up at five A.M. It was like a drug in me. As a traveler I can achieve a kind of high, a somewhat altered state of consciousness. I think it must be what athletes feel. I am transported out of myself, into another dimension in time and space. While the journey is on buses and across land, I begin another journey inside my head, a journey of memory and sensation, of past merging with present, of time growing insignificant.

My journey was now filled with dreams of other journeys to cool, breezy places. The plateaus of Tibet, the altiplano of Bolivia, cold places, barren, without tropical splendor. I did not dream of Africa and its encompassing heat. I longed for white Siberia, for Tierra del Fuego, the Arctic tundra, vast desolate plains. I longed for what came next. Whatever the next stop, the next love, the next story might be.

Josh was sitting in the back of the truck when it pulled up to my pension. "I thought you were going to Guatemala City," I said.

"Well," he said, smiling, "there are other ways to get to Panama." He grabbed my duffel and pulled me on. Then we sat across from each other as we set out through a lush pass in the mountains, bouncing in the back through a very misty morning, past charging rivers, herds of cattle and goats, toward the border of Honduras.

At about five-thirty the driver stopped to pick up two women. They were teachers who worked in one-room schoolhouses in the hills. One of them told us she walked an hour from where the truck would drop her to her school and she did this twice a day every day.

"You must be exhausted every day," I said.

She had a bright smile, sleek black hair, and dark eyes. "Oh, no." She laughed. "The walk is beautiful and I always arrive feeling refreshed."

"You never get tired of it?" I asked, incredulous.

"There is always something to see," she said, smiling. At six-thirty, she got off, heading toward the mountains, waving, then disappeared along a trail.

At seven we reached the frontier and found it closed. We took our bags, waved good-bye to our pickup, and waited for the border to open and for some other vehicle, which we assumed would materialize, to appear. For an hour or so we clomped around, taking pictures of an enormous cow that was nearby. At last the border opened. "You want to go into Honduras?" the guard said with a bit of a sneer.

"Yes, we're going to the ruins." I have no idea why I felt the need to say that, but I did.

"Well, if you want to go into Honduras, that's your problem." He stamped our passports just as another minibus arrived, heading for Copán.

We spent the day at the ruins. We had no plan, really, no sense of whether we would stay there or try to get out of the jungle and to some city by night. The ruins were fairly deserted and we spent the day climbing around. We had not gone far when we startled an enormous blue-black snake that had been asleep. The snake rose up on its side, then chased us along the path for several feet. I had never been chased by a snake before and was amazed at how fast it could move. Josh hurled a stone at it and the snake disappeared into the jungle.

We walked deeper into the jungle and a wasp stung me twice on the knee. Josh scooped wet mud and packed it around the bites. My knee became very stiff and I thought I couldn't go on, but he coaxed me and I did.

We came to a pyramid. It was hardly excavated. The steps were broken, stones were covered with moss, but we climbed. My knee hurt, but I didn't care. We climbed and climbed. It was a very high pyramid and when we reached the top, we were silent. We sat still on the top of this unexcavated pyramid, looking at the tremendous jungle that stretched before us.

I liked Josh. What more can I say. I liked him. I wanted to go with him to Panama. I had only just met him and I hadn't thought it through, but I wanted to go. Thinking about it now, I'm not sure what it was that I liked about him so much — he was, in fact, rather ordinary — but I think it had something to do with the fact that he was an American. He was an intelligent American male and he represented for me all those things that were now missing in my life. He could have dinner with my parents at my father's club. The men would wear suits and ties and discuss the market over Scotch and soda. My mother would wink at me across the table. Later she'd take me aside and say what a nice man he was and how they hoped they'd be seeing more of him.

I thought about Alejandro, sitting in that dark apartment, waiting for my return, telegram in hand, but all I could think about was going on with Josh to Panama. That afternoon as we walked, we spoke of more personal things. I told him I had a boyfriend in Mexico City. He said he had just broken up with a woman in Berkeley.

We checked into the Mayan Copán and had dinner on the patio. Sitting there with Josh in the steam of the jungle brought back to me what until now had seemed farthest away — the hot summer days and nights of Manhattan. Suddenly I found myself longing for a dripping ice cream cone while the plaintive song of a saxophonist echoed up the avenue. I longed for the heat of the pavement, cheap wine during a concert in the park, and black children jumping double-Dutch while illegal aliens sold assorted ices —pineapple, anise, coconut. I wanted to be transplanted, to feel the pace of the city in summer — an afternoon spent at the matinee, a weekend flight to Jones Beach. I even longed for what repulsed me — the garbage, the stench of urine, the homeless, the yellow smogged sky. All the things I swore I'd never miss.

After dinner we sat on the porch of the hotel, drinking rum and Cokes and speaking of our travels. Josh told me about trekking through Afghanistan and hiking across the Khyber Pass, about wanting to walk to Turkistan and getting captured by rebels somewhere along the way. He said that he had talked his way into and out of every situation you could imagine. "But if I were a woman," he said, "I don't know if I'd do it alone."

"It has its ups and downs," I said.

"Have you ever had anything bad happen to you?"

I shrugged. "Some near-misses, that's all."

He sipped his rum contemplatively. "I've heard terrible stories."

"Like what?"

He leaned over and kissed me on the lips. "I don't want to ruin your evening."

"You may as well tell me now."

He pulled his chair closer. "Well, this happened to a friend of a friend of mine. Not someone I really know. I met him once, that's all. I'm not even sure it happened the way my friend said. This man went to Turkey with his wife. To Istanbul. He never talks about it, but they went to Istanbul. It was a kind of second honeymoon. They wanted to start a family, so anyway, they went on this second honeymoon —"

I reached across, touching his hand. "Just tell me the story." He held onto my fingers and did not let go until he was done.

"All right. So they went. They were at the bazaar one day and his wife wanted to buy a dress. She was a pretty woman, blond. So they went into a store and after a while he got bored and said he wanted to take a walk. He said he'd go have a cigarette and be back in half an hour. They had a little fight about this, but he went anyway. When he came back, the dress shop was closed and no one was there. So he thought they'd closed early and he went to the hotel and waited for his wife to meet him there. But she never went back to the hotel. He waited and waited, but she never came back. He talked to the police and the next day they went to the shop, but the people, people he recognized from the day before, said they had never seen the woman and she'd never been there. He stayed in Istanbul for weeks, but they never found his wife."

"And he thinks she was kidnapped by the people who owned the dress shop?"

Josh nodded. "Kidnapped. And sold."

"Sold?"

"That's right. Sold."

We sat in silence for a long time, listening to the jungle noises. After a while, Josh pulled me by my hand. "Come on," he said. "Let's go to sleep."

In the morning we boarded the minibus. The women who got on all had holes cut in their dresses where their nipples hung out and small children suckled. The men carried machetes, which they checked with the bus driver by tucking them under his seat. Many of the men had slash marks on their arms or faces and many were missing fingers and limbs, so it appeared that this precaution was a necessary one. I was reminded of the movies about the Wild West, where the gunslingers check their guns at the saloon door.

Several hours later we reached La Entrada. Everyone there

carried a machete. We went to a bar to have a beer and a man walked in. Both his hands had been chopped off above the wrist and his nose was missing. "A machete did that," Josh said.

Suddenly I could not bear the thought of spending a moment alone. The story he had told me of the woman in Istanbul stayed in my mind and I knew that having heard it, I'd never be quite the same.

Josh was undecided about which direction he would take and I was undecided as to whether or not I would go with him. I wanted him to ask me. I thought that if he asked me, I'd go. From La Entrada there were buses to either coast and points east and west. The choices were infinite. But Josh had taken a liking to inland Honduras and the guidebook said there were some things to see in a neighboring town called Florida. "Look," Josh said. "How often are you going to be in this part of Honduras?"

"Not often," I said. And we hitched a ride with a farmer in the back of his pickup truck.

Josh had heard about a gas station attendant in Florida who knew everything there was to know about the Mayan ruins in the vicinity.

"I thought you were tired of ruins."

"Well, we're here. We may as well make the most of it."

We found the gas station attendant and he sent us in the direction of some ruins not far from the border. We crawled around in the heat of the day while Josh tried to decide what kind of people lived in this place. A dog that was skin and bones followed us. I threw him scraps of sandwich, but Josh kept trying to chase the dog away.

Later that night while a tropical breeze blew in through the windows of our small room, Josh told me he was going to go to Salvador. I thought to myself how, having lost all sense of proportion, I'd follow this man anywhere, and after about thirty seconds I said, "Mind if I come with you?"

"Not at all," he said. "But what about your boyfriend in Mexico?"

"What about him?"

"Well, won't he be upset?"

"Do you want me to go with you or not?" I asked, pressing the point.

"I want you to do whatever makes you happy," he said.

"Well, then I'm going with you."

He drifted right to sleep, but I stayed awake. I could not stop thinking about that woman he'd told me about the night before, a captive in some harem, a woman used and tossed aside, trying endlessly to plan her escape. A blonde among dark people. A woman who could not speak their tongue. Perhaps she had been ingenious, learning their ways, and had made a life for herself wherever her prison was. Perhaps she had fallen into the hands of a benevolent sheik who took pity on her, and though his pride would not permit him to release her, he would not abuse her, either.

But I think the scenario is much darker than this. That woman would never be free. She would never return. If it were me, when I realized that rescue wouldn't come, that I would not be found, that I would never go home and would always be a prisoner of men, I would lose my mind. I would die of grief or by my own hand.

In the morning we stood at the crossroads at La Entrada, waiting for the bus for Salvador. Until the bus arrived, I wasn't sure what I was going to do, but as soon as I saw it, kicking up dust, puffing in the distance, I knew what lay before me. When the driver stopped and opened the ancient door, I kissed Josh. "Have a safe journey," I said.

"What? Aren't you coming?"

"I'm going to Tegucigalpa." If he begs me, I told myself, I'll go.

"Well, whatever suits you."

He wasn't begging. He wasn't even asking. "Yes, I guess this suits me." I waved good-bye. Sitting on my duffel in the sun — though dreaming of the way I could have gone with him — I felt sure I was on the right road. About an hour later the bus for Tegucigalpa approached. The bus driver asked me if I was a *gente de la sandía*, a watermelon person. A joke on the Sandinistas, and I said no, I was a tourist from the United States. He nodded and I took a seat in the rear.

It was a big bus this time, heading for the capital. Not long after I boarded a young girl and her father got on, and they sat near the front. After about an hour the bus stopped and the father got off. He kissed his daughter good-bye and waved as the bus drove away. The girl was perhaps thirteen or fourteen and after a few moments she began to cry. She cried uncontrollably and the driver stopped. Women rushed to her, then came away shaking their heads. She was an idiot, one of the women told me. Her father had abandoned her here on this bus. "Too expensive to feed," the man behind me muttered. "Too expensive to keep."

In Tegucigalpa, exhausted and beginning to come down with a cold, I checked into a fairly expensive hotel, the Prado, for sixteen dollars. I was promised hot water, which was why I took the room. Upstairs, I unpacked, relaxed, and went to shower. There was no water at all. I called downstairs and waited for an endless period of time until they told me that none of the rooms on my floor had water and that I should move to another floor.

I wended my way lower and lower into the bowels of the hotel, in search of water, past broken windows, shrieking children, rooms above nightclubs and bars, past a parrot that kept screaming in Spanish, "Take out the garbage," into a kind of dungeonlike darkness of windowless basement rooms until I met a man whose mother had died in Madrid that morning and he had water and let me shower in his room. The man was very nice and I took the room next to his, a cheaper room than where I'd started, where I rested in this now dreary place, listening through the walls to the man whose mother had died, trying to get his call through to Madrid.

8

THE LAND OF THE DEAD

As I JOURNEY BACK FROM HONDURAS, I THINK OF my parents and try to make sense of the past. I wonder what has brought me from a small town in Illinois to what has now become my life. I imagine myself in other scenarios. Suburban housewife, veterinarian, porno queen. This one I am living feels more viable, though I have no idea how it came to be. I wander the world, drifting between places and people. All I ever wanted was consistency, a kind of coherent life. What I have is flux.

I do not understand my relations with men. I have searched for love, yet always find those men who cannot love. These are the ones I care for with a deep passion. And the others, those who could love me, I mold into friends. I know I am not the only woman in the world who does this. I know many women who do the same.

My parents knew each other for six weeks before they married. He was forty-four. She was thirty-four. Neither of them ever thought they'd marry, though they were both attractive and could have married many times. They were brought together by a gypsy. A woman who told my father, who had been away from Chicago for many years, that he would be called home by his brother and meet a woman through him. It was not long after the gypsy told him this that my father received a letter from his brother, pleading him to come and work with him.

My mother worked in the lingerie department at Saks. She had gone to grammar school with the wife of my father's brother, the woman who would soon become my aunt. My aunt stopped in to return a peach nightgown that my uncle had given her as a present. She recognized my mother. My mother once told me that she thought the nightgown would have looked very good on my aunt and that it was just a whim that made her return it. If my aunt had kept the gown, my mother says, I never would have been born.

It was not long after that that my father called. He said he had been going through the pants he was sending to the cleaners and found her number, which my aunt had stuffed into his pocket. Would she like to have dinner? When she walked out the door that evening, she told my grandmother that if she didn't like him, she would be home at ten. At nine-thirty my father said he was tired and would she mind if he brought her home. When she walked in the door, my grandmother was dismayed. "Oh, you didn't like him."

"On the contrary," my mother replied, "that's the man I'm going to marry."

Six weeks later she did. I was born exactly a year and a month after the wedding. They hardly knew one another at all when I was born. They learned about each other through having me. In the process of learning, they argued. Quarrels about lights being left on, dishes in the sink. My father longed for the neat, ordered, empty life of his bachelorhood. He could not stand the disorder of a family, the disarray children brought with them. And my mother, in this house of conflict, recognized the home life she'd thought she'd left behind.

To alleviate all this tension, I was the perfect child. I was obedient and cheerful, disciplined and polite. Unlike my younger brother, I did everything right. I played the piano, had many friends, got straight A's. I kept order and knew how to get out of the path of an oncoming tornado. I knew exactly how to break my bread and put away dishes to thwart a fight. But I was also leading a secret life.

I'd go to prom with the nice Jewish boy whose family belonged to our temple, then sneak off on school nights with the leader of a Puerto Rican gang. I'd make faces at my mother's cigarettes and smoke marijuana in the garage. I wrote thank-you notes, kept an accurate birthday book, twirled the baton on Flag Day, marched with pompons in the homecoming parade. I also stole car keys, slid down drain pipes, slipped off to the beach for a night of bonfires, beer, and adolescent boys.

No one could fault me. No one knew that underneath my propriety I was boiling over. On the surface I gave my parents whatever they wanted. I was a demilitarized zone, the buffer between them. I let them try to love each other through me. But beneath it all, I was plotting my escape, and when the time came, I was gone.

When I returned alone to Alejandro's barren walls, his cold, lifeless apartment, only two days late, there was no sign of him anywhere. The laundry that hung on the line felt as if it had been dry for days. There was no food in the refrigerator. No sign of life. No soup or cold chicken, which wasn't like him. No note of greeting. He wasn't expecting me. Yet here I was, where I had no desire to be.

I waited. At about ten o'clock Marta arrived, looking miserable. "Oh, these buses. I can't stand it. Every week, the same thing. What are you doing here? Alejandro said he had no idea when you'd be back. We thought you'd be gone for months."

"I was gone for a few weeks," I reminded her, feeling hurt that my absence wasn't long enough.

"Yes, well, we didn't think you'd be back yet, that's all."

"Well, here I am," I said.

A few minutes later the door opened and Alejandro walked in with his brother, Ruben. Ruben had his saxophone in hand and it was clear they'd been drinking. They were laughing as they came in, then looked surprised to see me. "María," Alejandro said, rushing to me. He kissed me on the cheek. "You are back. What a surprise."

"Yes, here I am," I said again, wondering what I was doing here. "You didn't get my cable."

"No," he said.

"I can't believe you didn't get my cable." I thought how I could have gone with Josh all the way to Panama. On the other hand, it had been my choice not to.

"This is Mexico" was his reply.

For the next few days Alejandro and I hardly spoke to each

other. At night we drifted to opposite ends of the bed. I was distracted and wanted to leave. But for some reason I found I couldn't be alone, even if it meant only going through the motions of being with someone.

After several days he said, "So, María, tell me. Is there someone else? Did you meet someone on your last journey?"

"I didn't meet anyone," I lied.

"Why is it so hard for me to believe you?"

"Look," I told him. "I really care for you."

"I know you met someone. You are not the same person who left a few weeks ago."

I debated telling him the truth, but it didn't make much sense, really. Josh was not someone who was going to be important in my life and Alejandro was someone I cared for, and I saw no reason to hurt him. But as I sat there in his apartment that evening, staying up late, smoking cigarettes and drinking beer, I wondered just what it was I was doing with my life. "Where will you ever find a man who will take care of you the way I do?" he said.

"Alejandro," I replied, "I am glad you take care of me. I appreciate it."

In truth, I was bored with it. I had been with men where I had to do all the work and I had hated that. I had been with men who didn't care and wouldn't lift a finger. But the opposite wasn't very satisfying, either, and I felt in my relationship with him more like a man than a woman.

"But I want something more equal. I want to share my life," I said.

Then he grew irate. "You don't know what you want, María. You say you want to share, but you don't do anything."

He was not entirely wrong about this, but he wasn't entirely right. "I do want to share, but we are very different. I come from a different culture."

He opened another beer. "You and your goddamn culture. You North Americans, you think you can just come down here with your dollars and take advantage of us."

I reached for his beer. "I am just trying to understand."

He pushed my hand away. "Fuck your understanding. Fuck all you gringos."

Later he came over and wrapped his arms around me. "I'm sorry," he said. "I love you."

"Don't drink so much," I told him.

He buried his head against my chest. I ran my hand through his thick black hair. "You know that I love you," he said.

Solitude became my profession, my calling, and what I did, I did alone. I practiced it as a physician practices his trade. I studied. I apprenticed. I developed expertise. I dwelled in these rooms with Alejandro and his stepmother, with the yellow TV, with books wrapped in brown paper, and could not find my own language anywhere. I lived with only one small, cracked mirror over the sink, and I could not find myself. Even when I was with Alejandro, I locked myself away. In my heart, at my core, I was alone.

I was surprised by my own skill. In New York, before departing, I had not been able to spend one minute alone, except to work. And as soon as it was done, I was out the door. I made frantic social dates with people I hardly knew and didn't care about. People who would invariably cancel, leaving me bereft and frightened by the prospect of solitude.

And now suddenly, unexpectedly, I turned inward. I encircled myself in solitude. I didn't know it at the time, but it was a kind of cloak around me. I convinced myself that it was language and culture that separated me from those around me. I did not need to go off into the woods, to the Arctic tundra, to a desert island. I was living in a city of eighteen million people, the most densely populated city of the world next to Tokyo, and I found that without much effort I could make myself completely alone.

I wanted to be near water, and thinking that perhaps we could patch things up, I suggested to Alejandro that we go to

Veracruz for the weekend. Veracruz was on the gulf; it was supposed to be like Havana before the revolution. On Saturday morning at five A.M. we were on the first bus out. By about eleven, we had arrived in this city of arcades, promenades, mosaics, Caribbean music, *mariscos*, men in guayaberas, and the sea. I was thrilled to be near water and we checked into a hotel. We were both very tired and so after a long walk around the town and a stop for a beer and lunch of ceviche with horseradish sauce, we wandered back to the hotel for a rest.

When I woke, it was raining. It was raining hard, so I went back to sleep, thinking that the storm would pass. But when I woke again later, the storm was worse. The wind whipped past buildings and the sky was black. We could see the sea from our window and the waves were extremely high. We never left our room that evening. We slept and read and waited, but the storm did not subside. I kept waking up, thinking I must talk to Alejandro. I must tell him what is wrong. But I couldn't bring myself to wake him. In truth there was nothing wrong except that he wanted me to marry him and spend my life in Mexico, and I was dreaming of some drifter I'd encountered on the Honduran border.

I dozed in and out of sleep until dawn. Then I looked out and saw nothing but water. No streets, no sidewalks, no cars.

I woke Alejandro. There must have been five feet of water on the ground and we were stuck in this flood. Alejandro said there was nothing to do but wait, so I read and slept for a few more hours. When I next looked out, the water was gone. This storm, we learned that morning, is called an *aguacero*, and it comes with the wind they call *El Norte*. It brings a flood like that, but the city has learned how to cope, and the streets and sidewalks have drainage holes that take the floods out to sea.

We went to breakfast at La Parroquia on the Plaza de Armas. The café had white tiled walls, fans, cement floors, waiters in white jackets, and served wonderful coffee and scrambled eggs. The day was sunny, and so after breakfast we went to the popular Mocambo Beach. We passed poor fishermen who lived on the shore in shanties and crazy, dangerous dogs who patrolled the shantytown. I could not imagine how these people made it through the storm that night.

On the beach Alejandro told me a story about his family. This story was a kind of missing link, the one that made me understand all the rest. He had a blind brother named Tomás. Blindness, he told me, was inherited through the women in his family. One day when he was small and all the children had gone out to play, his mother went into the street, leaving Tomás alone, and somehow his brother got on to the roof and fell off. Now, Alejandro told me, his brother lay in bed like a vegetable, as he had lain for twenty years, in his mother's house. He could not speak or move or see, and his every need had to be taken care of. Alejandro looked at me, his eyes filled with a rage I couldn't help thinking was directed at me. "It is her curse," he said. "It is what she deserves."

That afternoon we took the bus to La Antigua (old Veracruz). En route Alejandro reminded me of my history. "You know, this is where Cortés landed and it is also where your president, Woodrow Wilson, bombed our shipyards and killed two hundred of my people in order to quell a revolution."

"I didn't realize it was Veracruz," I told him.

"Yes," he said in a huff. "The conquered always recall their history better than the conqueror."

We reached the place where in 1519 Cortés had tied up his ships. The exact spot is a famous ceiba tree, a giant tree with enormous roots that reach into the walls of the city, the roots exposed. Centuries have passed. The walls have crumbled. Only the roots of the tree, which have endured, sustain the walls. Alejandro looked at the tree, and a satisfied grin came over his features. "You see," he said to me, "the walls are in ruins. Nothing has survived. Only the tree. It was here before Cortés. It will be here after."

On the bus ride back from the gulf, I made the mistake of referring to the time when I'd be going home. "Home?" Alejandro said. "I always thought you'd come to stay."

"I've always said I'm going home." At that moment, in fact, I ached to go home. I longed to get away. And yet I could not seem to leave. Even as I thought about it then, it seemed impossible that I would ever go home. Still I yearned to return. "I want to go home," I said.

"Yes, but I am in love with you. You may go, but I am in love with you." He held out his hands to show me how empty they were.

I shook my head and said I didn't think he was in love with me, but this only made him more angry. "How do you know what I am?" he said.

"I don't want to hurt you," I told him. "I love you, but I'm not in love with you." Even as I said it, I thought how much I had hated that distinction when men had made it to me. "I want to always be honest with you," I told him. "I could never stay here. I couldn't stay with you."

"I only want you, María. There is no one else for me." Alejandro could have had just about any Mexican woman of his social class. He was handsome, charming, kind, and loyal. Instead he had decided to fall in love with me, though I had told him this was not a good idea.

Alejandro, for all his kindness — and he was a very kind man — suffered from what I have come to call the Aztec complex. He was a stoical man of great dignity and pride. Stoical, stubborn, hiding behind a mask, basically disdaining women. He chose to involve himself with women like me, who would only make him feel bad about himself, or with women like Angelita, whom he could easily dominate, who did not interest him. Like Móctezuma, opening the gates of his city to embrace Cortés, Alejandro welcomed me to break his heart.

After being back in Mexico City for a few days, I wanted to go to San Miguel and decided to return. The morning of my departure as I packed, there was a knock at the door. When I opened it, I found a man standing there. He said he had a telegram for Alejandro Santiago Sanchez, and Alejandro opened it.

"What is it?" I asked. "Is it bad news?"

"It's from you," he said. And he handed me the cable I had sent weeks before from Guatemala City, which read simply, "Back Friday, Mary."

I HAD NEVER BEEN TO A PARTY AT A CEMETERY before, but Lupe said it would be fun. She wanted me to help her with the preparations and accompany her there. I wasn't sure what this entailed since Day of the Dead in America is essentially Halloween, so I asked if she wanted me to help her make costumes for the children. But she said no, it wasn't like that at all; if we could work in my kitchen, she would teach me.

Lupe brought over a giant cauldron and we began baking breads and small cakes. We shopped for cinnamon, pecans, brown sugar, flour, eggs, food coloring, colored sugars. In the cauldron, we put a kilo of sifted flour, ten eggs. We put in the grated cinnamon, the sugars, pecans. Then she made small cups and in the cups she put food coloring and she dyed the dough. Then her hand shaped the dough. She made little lambs and elephants, reindeer and skulls, coffins and flowers. I watched as she carved skulls, shaped coffins, wove funereal wreaths with her colored dough.

Death was everywhere for days. In town all the stores were selling the little cakes and cookies, sugar candy and funereal wreaths, and everyone was laughing and happy and having a wonderful time. The night before we went to the cemetery, we stayed up, making another batch of breads. I asked Lupe how she had learned to be such a good cook and she told me she had carefully watched the patrones she had worked for and remembered what they did. Even though she could not read recipes, she could remember.

"I remember everything," she told me. And suddenly she began to cry. She broke down and sobbed into her apron. Another one of José Luis's women was pregnant, and Lupe was pregnant, and she remembered everything, all the good and all the bad, and it was all rolled into one. "I am sick of all these men," she said. "If I didn't have so many children, if it weren't for this" — she patted her belly — "I'd get away from them all." She said José Luis had told her that afternoon that if she went to the movies alone — or went out anywhere alone — it meant only one thing. That she was looking for a man. He said that if she did that, he would kidnap Pollo and take her to one of his other señoras. "How can I look for a man like this? He doesn't even want me anymore," she said, "but he threatens me."

Lupe said she was a slave to that man and she'd been a slave to the man before him. "Don't ever be a slave," she told me. "Be free. Always be free." Then she apologized for crying and we went back to shaping our skulls, our tiny coffins.

Mexico is the land in which Xochipilli, the young god of beauty, love, and youth, was depicted with a death's head contorted into the most hideous of smiles. Life to the Aztecs came only from death. One flowed naturally into the other. The people who worshiped Xipe Totec, god of vegetation, watched as their priests flayed victims alive and walked around in their warm skins. Children still play with puppets called Dead Mariachi or Dead Peasant or even Dead Dead Man. To be Mexican means to be well acquainted with birth and death.

The cemetery in San Miguel is about an hour's walk outside of town and I'd never been there before that day. We left early in the morning, Lupe, me, and all of the children except María Elena, who was pregnant and not feeling well. We carried our flowers and baskets of food. Lupe had a dear friend, she told me, who had died the year before, and she also had a child who had been born dead. We would go to their graves.

The cemetery was alive with people, flowers, and streamers. Families gardened around graves, pulling up weeds, planting flowers. Everyone was eating cookies and cakes, drinking coffee or tequila, passing food around. The festivities were everywhere except for in a small enclosed area near the middle of the cemetery. I asked Lupe what it was. She said she didn't know, so I went over. It was the American part, all fenced in, well gardened and kept up, but with no visitors, no one bringing flowers. It seemed lonely and sad. "Lupe," I said, "if I die here, will you be sure I am buried in the Mexican part of the cemetery?"

She laughed. "It is sad over there, isn't it."

Suddenly it became very important to me that she make this promise. "Promise me," I said. "I won't be buried in the American part."

She squeezed my arm. "I promise, but you won't die in Mexico."

We reached the grave of Lupe's friend. Two of Lupe's other friends, sisters named Carmen and Consuela, were clearing a nearby grave, scrubbing the tombstone. They had a large picnic basket with them and offered us some slices of chicken and a beer. I wasn't hungry, but I understood that it would offend them if I refused. They seemed very content. Both had strange, witchlike faces. Carmen had clear green eyes, unusual for a Mexican, and silver hair down to her waist. After a while she began to talk about the grave she was clearing. "It is my son's," she said. "And my mother." She looked at Consuela. "Our mother." Consuela nodded.

"Oh, your son," I mumbled.

"And our mother," Consuela said, as if she were proud of this fact.

"Yes, my son was killed last year. With an ice pick in his head." She said this as if she were telling me about a new movie she'd seen.

"And our mother died of grief, six weeks later," Consuela said. It was like a routine the two of them had worked up together.

"So we buried them together. We have just put the tombstone in. It is very nice, I think, don't you?"

Lupe said she thought it was very nice and for a while we

all admired the tombstone. They insisted that we touch the cool reddish-gray stone, run our fingers over the carved letters, look at our reflections in its polished surface. Then they offered us some little cakes and Lupe offered them some of ours. They admired the basket Lupe had brought. "These are beautiful." And they took a coffin and skull and offered them to their dead.

"You don't eat them?" I asked.

"Some do. I prefer to offer them," Carmen replied. "So" — she grinned at me — "if you die in Mexico, you will be buried there." She pointed to the American enclave.

Lupe laughed, knowing I was being teased. "Oh, no," Lupe said as if on cue. "She will be here with us."

Then Lupe wanted to find the grave of her stillborn child. She had an idea of where it was, but as we walked to the children's part of the cemetery, she became confused. The grave was unmarked and more graves had appeared since she'd last been there, and she couldn't find it.

Instead we cleared away the weeds on the grave of an unknown child. We planted the pansies and a small rose sprig we had brought with us. We knew that the rose sprig would not live without care, but we planted it anyway. Then we sat beside the grave and ate avocado sandwiches. A priest came by and blessed the grave with holy water from a pill bottle.

In the far corner of the cemetery a bonfire burned, but Lupe didn't want to get near the fire. I asked her what it was. "They are burning the coffins of those who could no longer pay to stay there." She asked if I would help her make a bank account. She said she never wanted them to burn her coffin. "All right," I said. "I won't let them burn your coffin if you don't let them bury me where the Americans are." We shook hands, sealing our pact, both laughing at the thought of our impending doom.

Toward the end of the day some people began to leave while others dragged out more beer and bottles of tequila; for them the festivities would continue into the night. Lupe was ready to leave so we said good-bye to Carmen and Consuela. They asked if she'd be back that night, but she said no.

As we walked back across the fields, I asked her why she wouldn't return that night, but she shook her head. "It is one thing to go in the day," she mumbled. "It's another to go at night."

That night I returned and found the cemetery transformed. It was a blaze of fires and strange dances, of drunk men staggering and women incanting. Candles burned on tombstones. Odd shadows illumined the faces of the living. I passed Consuela and Carmen, their faces even more witch-like now, glowing red in the flames. I waved, but they did not see me. I stopped beside them, but they did not recognize me. Carmen rocked back and forth, her silver hair glistening as if on fire. Death masks abounded and skeletons marched. The ghosts were on parade.

I journey among the dead, wandering from grave to grave. Flames dance in the shine of tombstones. Dancers try to pull me into their dance. A young man appears before me, thrusting a bottle into my hand. He insists that I drink. I drink as if from a well. When I go to hand him the bottle, the boy is gone and an old woman is there. Her hair is pure white, her eyes flashes of silver. She breathes on me and my body is warmed. She looks at me through an eye of glass. She tells me my name and where I am from. She whispers the name of the person I last loved. "Who are you?" I say.

But she says nothing. Instead she leads me somewhere and I follow. Around us the dancers dance. I feel the heat of the flames. The drunk get drunker. We pass the American part of the cemetery and it is quiet and still. I walk quickly, following the old woman, her hair like a trail of moonlight on water. I do not know where we are going but she beckons to me. Then she stops. She extends her arms, opens her skirts. She covers the ground. I am the mother you never had, she tells me. I am the daughter you will one day be. I can make nothing of her gibberish. Instead I curl into her arms.

I wake to find myself lying on a small grave, a rose sprig above my head, about to blossom.

When I returned, Globo began acting strangely. She lurked in closets, pulling out socks, making piles with my clothes. Her body shook; her legs trembled. It wasn't long before one kitten was born. It slipped out, its sack intact, and Globo bit it free. I rushed over to Lupe and told her to come and bring the children because Globo was having kittens. Lupe came with Lisa and Pollo and Pancha. Word spread through the neighborhood that Globo, the balloon cat, was having kittens.

Other children from San Antonio arrived. They brought Cokes and small cakes. They wore rags, tattered trousers. They were filthy. They sat in silence around the cardboard box as Globo produced six kittens. More children came. One of them brought a box of piglets his sow had just had. I made guacamole and went to the store for chips and more soda. Globo sat in her box, quietly nursing her kittens, while Pancha the lamb watched, and the children drank Cokes and ate guacamole, and three piglets ran around.

We were all happy. Later, when I was leaving San Miguel for the last time, Lupe would recall that day and say how happy we were.

THE APARTMENT NEXT TO MINE HAD BEEN VACANT for a while, but suddenly the tenants returned. Two women appeared who had been at an archaeological dig in the jungle, and one of them was sick. The sick woman, who had run a road crew in Canada, was big and bony and powerful with long dishwater-blond hair. Her name was Rosalind and her roommate was Anna. "She picked up something in the jungle," Anna said. "She has paratyphoid, according to the doctors in Querétaro." In Querétaro there is a five hundred thousand dollar blood-separating machine that tells you what tropical disease you have contracted.

Rosalind looked pretty bad. There was something about seeing a woman that strong with that flushed, feverish look, and I thought to myself, "This woman could die." Someone had to give Rosalind a shot three times a day and Trevor volunteered. He practiced on a few oranges and soon he was giving Rosalind shots. I told her that if she needed anything, if she was sick, just to holler for me. I was home writing most of the days.

Soon after Rosalind and Anna were settled, a Mexican woman came to my door. She had two scrawny children who seemed to be suffering from malnutrition. She asked for work and I told her I had none. Then she begged me. "Please, please." She pointed to her children, their bellies distended. I said she could clean and I'd give her some money and lunch.

While the woman was cleaning, Lupe came by. "Who is that woman?" she asked indignantly.

"It's just for the day."

But she looked very hurt and upset. "If you need someone to work for you, I will do it."

"It's just for the day," I told her. "The woman needed something to eat." Lupe went away, looking very sad.

The woman ate lunch standing up in the kitchen while I sat at the table on the patio. I watched her standing at the sink, eating rice and chicken, handing bits of food wrapped in tortilla to her children, while I sat at the table, comfortable and alone.

Alejandro was supposed to arrive Friday after work, but he never did. I saw Lupe Saturday morning and she asked where he was. I told her he hadn't come. "Do you think he has left me?" I asked her, unsure myself how I felt about this.

"No," she said. "I doubt it. Something may have happened. You never can tell. You have no phone. There is no way to reach you." Then she grinned at me. "Or maybe he did drop you."

On Sunday I went over to Lupe's. She invited me into her kitchen and I sat down. She saw I was sad and I was about to talk to her about it. Just then Pollo squatted down and spilled a bloody diarrhea all over the ground. "My god," I shouted, "Lupe, is she sick? What should we do?"

Lupe just shrugged. "I've had her to the doctor. She just does that. It is the water. There's nothing we can do."

Seeing Pollo get sick like that did not make me want to talk about my small problems, but I did not know where to turn. It was Lupe who raised the issue. "That Mexican, has he disappeared?" I got tears in my eyes. I realized how much I hated being alone again. "You know," she said, "men are not worth it. I don't know how to tell you this, but they just are not worth it. We think they are, but they aren't. Other things are worth it, but not men."

Lupe was cleaning up after Pollo and I could not bring myself to look. "You know," she went on, "I met José Luis in a bar. I hardly knew anything about him, but we started to be together. I don't know what I feel for him, but he gives me fifty pesos a day. The señora gives me two hundred pesos a month, plus this house, to feed my children. I can't feed my kids without his money. So I don't throw him out." She paused and looked at me. "But a woman has got to make it on her own. No one is going to help you. No one. Don't cry for a man, especially a man who needs other women. No woman needs a man like that. And I'm not sure you need a man. Anyway, don't ever cry for one," she said to me. "They are never worth it."

Then I asked Lupe if she'd like to work for me. I had not wanted to ask her this, but now I did. I told her I could pay her two hundred pesos a week and we could help each other out. She said, "As long as we stay friends." I told her we would stay friends.

As I was leaving, Lupe told me not to worry. "Someone is watching out for you," she said.

That night as I sat at dinner with my window open I heard a voice call to me. I listened and thought I heard it say, "I love you." Lupe came in a few moments later and she heard it, too. Then Globo came and sat on my windowsill and stared at me. I gave her a piece of chicken which she ate slowly, methodically. I gave her another. She was a beautiful gray cat with big green eyes. "I think Globo is a bruja," Lupe said. "A witch. A white witch, a good witch." My *nahual*, the Aztecs would say, the animal god come to protect me. I thought of my dream about the cat but said nothing more.

I settled into loneliness once again. The rhythm of my days and nights, the absence of real friends in San Miguel, all of this made me miss Alejandro more. Days passed and he did not return. I was beside myself with worry and with the tremendous sense that I had been abandoned. I did not know how to reach him. He had no phone. I called his school once and was told he was on sick days.

One morning as I was sitting down to work, I heard a loud banging at my door and a thick Virginian accent calling my name. "Hello, Mary, are you there? I know you are. Open up. I can hear you working."

Since there were no telephones and the only way to

contact someone was to pay a visit, I had to open the door and let Derek in. "Boy," he said, "I had a tough time tracking you down." Sweat dripped from his thick blond hair. His face was red. "Nobody lives all the way over here in San Antonio. You should move into the center of town, where the action is."

I told him I liked the quiet and asked if there was something I could do for him. He said I could invite him in and give him a cup of coffee, which I did. "I wrote some short stories." He held out a pile of papers. "I thought I'd get your impression of them. Would you take a look?"

"Sure, I'll stop by your place after I've read them."

He hesitated, as if somehow I hadn't gotten the point. "Well, I'm sort of anxious to send them out. I thought you'd be a good person."

"Sure, why don't I stop by tonight?" But it dawned on me that he wanted me to read them right then and there. "You want me to read them now? With you sitting here?" He said that's what he wanted. "Well," I said, "I was sort of working."

"It won't take that long," he said, making himself comfortable on the couch.

I read the stories, which were competent but uninspired, without the flare of his late-night tequila-induced tales of bullfights and suicidal dogs. I gave him some perfunctory advice and told him where to send them. He seemed satisfied because after about an hour or so, he got up. "Oh, by the way, your neighbor, what's her name, Laura," he said as he was leaving. "She was out on her balcony when I came by —"

"Rosalind," I corrected him.

"Yeah, she asked me to come and get you." I told him she was very sick. "Yeah, she didn't look so good."

"You've been here over an hour. You didn't think to tell me this before?"

He shrugged. "She just said to tell you to come over."

I rushed over to Rosalind's and found her in her bed,

trembling, covered with sweat. "What is it?" I asked her. "What's wrong?"

"Oh, it's nothing," she said. "It's just the flies." She swatted at the air. "Could you kill the flies? They keep bothering me. There's so many of them."

I looked around the room and didn't see a single fly. "Sure, Rosalind," I said, "I'll kill them. Anything else?"

"Yes," she said. "Look at this. Do you think something is wrong?" She raised her nightgown, displaying for me her sturdy, massive road-crew body with one of its organs, which I recognized as the spleen, protruding like a giant grapefruit from her side. I am not an expert on tropical diseases but I did know enough to know that an enlarged spleen, fever, and delirium were symptoms of malaria, not the paratyphoid that the five hundred thousand dollar blood-separating machine in Querétaro told us to treat her for.

"Rosalind," I said, "you sit tight. I'm going to get some help."

It was the one time I can really say Trevor came through. I ran home and told him I thought Rosalind had malaria and that it looked as if her spleen could rupture if we didn't do something about it. Trevor said his friend T.C. — the man who'd been branded—had a truck, and in less than an hour Trevor and T.C. arrived with the truck. I had gone into town to phone the American-British Hospital in Mexico City to warn them that Rosalind was being brought in.

While Anna, who'd rushed home from school, got Rosalind comfortable in the truck, I talked with T.C. about where he should take her, but mainly I looked at the brand. It was a deep, burnt cavern in his flesh with his own initials, TC. As they were ready to pull out, I said to him, "I heard somebody did that to you."

He shook his head. "Somebody did it for me. I paid someone to put that on my arm."

"You paid someone to brand you?"

"I had something to prove." He smiled. They drove off with Rosalind to Mexico City. Two days later they were back. Rosalind did have malaria; they'd put her on quinine, and she would be fine.

I ran into Derek in town a few nights later. "You know that woman, Rosalind, she almost died. I can't believe you didn't think to tell me right away."

"You know what your problem is?" Derek replied. "You need to lighten up. You take life too seriously." He patted me on the cheek, then walked away.

LUPE CAME OVER ONE MORNING AND FOUND ME crying upstairs. She said it was no good to cry over a man. "Cry over something important," she said. I told her I was crying over my work, but she shook her head. "Women only cry over men."

I went downstairs a little while later and she was doing the dishes. I asked her how many men she had had. She blushed and pretended she did not know what I was talking about. "I don't understand your accent," she said. So I asked her again how many men she had had and again she laughed. She said two, then she said twenty. Then she said, "I've lost count. And you, María?"

I said I had also lost count, but that I only wanted one.

"José Luis, you know, he has many women. He has three other women, but he lives with me. He has ten children with one, six with another. I think he has twenty-two in all, but he cannot remember how many children he has. But now there are more on the way. With women, you know," she said, "it is different. I was with one man for fifteen years. Then he left me with the three oldest and went to the border. I haven't seen him since."

"I hate it when men abandon me," I told her.

She laughed. "That is the way men are. Men are wanderers. Maybe you are a little like a man, María. You seem to be a wanderer as well."

I thought about what she had just said. "No, I want to be with one person in one place."

"We all want that," Lupe said. "Every woman wants that. But still you are a wanderer."

When Alejandro still did not appear, I decided to go to Mexico City to try to find him. I knew it was stupid for me to do this, but I could stand it no longer. I got the six A.M. bus and reached the Terminal Central del Norte by eleven. I took a taxi and pounded on his door. There was no one home and his top lock, for which I had no key, was locked. His landlord came out and asked what I wanted. I told him that Alejandro had disappeared, and he looked at me mockingly and laughed, giving me the feeling that he'd seen women doing this before. I wrote a note, which I slipped under the door, begging him to come to San Miguel or cable me with a message.

I went to Denny's, where I had an orange juice, listened to Muzak, and felt sorry for myself. I ran through my mind all that had happened in the past few months. I seemed compelled to, search, even though I had the sense — a slight, gnawing sense — that somehow I already had what I was looking for. I just couldn't recognize it. It was there in front of me, like when you search the house for your keys or your comb, which are on the dresser all along. Suddenly I felt almost driven, and I had to go back to San Miguel.

At the terminal, a man with cut-off legs moved on a kind of shoe that held his stumps. He sold crucifixes. Other people sold Kleenex, Chiclets, postcards. Everyone was trying to sell something just to get by. If you go under in Mexico, you go under. I couldn't imagine how a man with stumps could sell crucifixes and live, but life went on somehow in this place.

The bus was filled with Venezuelan firemen who were on their way to a convention in Guanajuato. The firemen were chain-smoking and they wouldn't let me open a window to get some air. It was terribly hot on the bus and I grew irritable. After about an hour and a half the bus driver and ticket taker pulled over and got off the bus. There was a restaurant at the side of the road and they went inside. I sat in the bus and waited. Soon the firemen grew irritable also. They honked the horn. They got off the bus and found the driver and ticket taker eating a leisurely lunch. We asked them what they thought they were doing and they pointed to their watches, indicating it was their hour for *comida*. We screamed at them, but they didn't care.

It was dark when I reached San Miguel. After trudging up the long alleyway home, I found my house redolent with the smell of coriander, beans, and sweet fish. From the light of the kitchen, I saw Alejandro chopping vegetables with a sharp knife. "Where have you been?" I said.

He told me that the previous week his father, who lived in San Luis Potosí, had had an accident with some arsenic at work. Alejandro had gone to help him out. He had asked Ruben to cable me, but his brother had forgotten. Alejandro said it was a *falta de comunicación*. And besides, he said, "I did not think it mattered to you, really, whether I came back or not."

"Well, it did matter. It does," I said.

"So, I am here."

Later we sat down to the dinner he had made. A special fish stew, rice, and beans. The fish took hours to prepare and is usually served only on special occasions like Christmas. While we were eating, the windows were open. It was a beautiful, cool night and Globo sat on the window ledge — her kittens whining for her on the ground below — watching over us.

9

ALONG THE COAST

I GREW RESTLESS AGAIN AS THE WEEKS WENT BY, and it wasn't long before I found myself en route back to Honduras to the Bay Islands off the coast, where the Carib people were black and everyone spoke English. It was the first English I'd heard spoken in many months and the change amazed me. I spent a day resting in San Pedro Sula, having traveled from Tegucigalpa by bus, and was setting out for La Ceiba and the ferryboat to Roatán.

At the bus station a child with a clubfoot dragging behind her came begging, barefoot, and I was sure her parents had sent her out to beg, but I couldn't refuse. I gave her money and bought her some cakes and fruit. Everywhere people sold contraband. Wrist watches, radios, Jockey shorts. A black woman stood with two children. One was crying, and the black woman kept beating her with her purse. An enormous black woman with a bandanna around her head walked by and began beating the woman who was beating the child. A small riot broke out.

Finally the doors of the bus opened and the black women in their red-checkered turbans pushed and shoved. I managed to get a seat on this bus, having failed to get one on the seven-thirty bus. I could not bear the thought of standing up for three hours in this heat which, even in the early morning hours, was already completely unbearable, and I felt I'd faint if the bus did not move.

At last it pulled out and a breeze blew in. People in the back of the bus were singing. We drove through miles and miles of banana plantations and fruit farms, mostly, I am certain, owned by United Fruit. Honduras is a true Banana Republic, and most of its agriculture is owned by American economic interests. I recalled lines from Neruda: "Among the bloodthirsty flies, the Fruit Company lands its ships, taking off the coffee and the fruit." I stared out the window as we drove by. The trees that lined the road were filled with buzzards.

At one o'clock, hot and hungry, we reached La Ceiba, and the bus driver let a few passengers disembark at the dock. With my South American guidebook open to the page that said, "Ferries leave regularly from the dock at La Ceiba to Roatán and the other islands," I walked slowly toward the lapping water along the rotting wood pier, the lifeless wharf, the absence of anything resembling a ferryboat.

A young couple, the same guidebook opened to the same page, stared forlornly at the same deserted dock, where we were the only signs of life. "This doesn't look very promising," the man said. We introduced ourselves. Andrew was a tall, very attractive attorney from San Francisco, and his girlfriend, Becky, was a biologist. "We've come a long way," he said.

"So have I." They were also trying to get to the Bay Islands and said they'd be glad to go with me to Roatán if we could find a way.

It was clear that there had been no regular-service ferry in years, and we were contemplating the prospect of turning around and traveling overland back across Honduras when a little man in a white linen suit, drenched in sweat, seemed to materialize out of nowhere. "Hello, I'm Charlton Jenks." He held out his hand. "Glad to meet you. I'm from Los Angeles. Researching a screenplay." He saw us, fingers pressed into our guidebooks. I had a feeling immediately that he stood at this dock all day, waiting for the misdirected like us. "No boats for the *islas* from here," he said. "Somebody ought to write those guys in England. Tell them there aren't any ferries. Everyone who comes overland and wants to get to the islands has the same problem. Hasn't been a regular ferry in a decade. If you don't mind waiting around until Sunday, you might find a boat to take you."

Sunday was three days away and La Ceiba didn't look like the kind of place where you'd want to spend three days.

"Is there any other way to get there?" Andrew asked.

"Oh, there are ways. I know a place we can go for lunch. Why don't we relax and discuss it at our leisure over a nice plate of rice and beans."

Charlton took my bag and we followed him, shrugging at each other, not sure what else to do. Over lunch Charlton Jenks — former band leader, TV and radio director, real estate developer, novelist whose *Mayan Magic* was made into a film by MGM — said that he was working on a screenplay of his last novel, which would be the first movie set in Honduras. He had been doing research in La Ceiba for the past five years. Andrew, Becky, and I glanced at one another with looks that formed our friendship, each of us trying to imagine spending half a decade of our lives in La Ceiba. "I've got a friend," he said. "A pilot. He'll get you to Guanaja. Owns half the island. You should go to the airport. I'll go with you. See if we can't get him to fly us to Guanaja."

We finished our lunch and Charlton dug around in his pockets for money. "Damn it," he said. "I've gotta go to the bank and cash a check." So he suggested we follow him to the bank and he'd cash a check, but when we got to his bank he had left his checkbook on Guanaja. "Must have left it in my hotel room there." He said he'd pay us back if we'd just front him the money to the island. We were beginning to get suspicious of him and we had already gotten out of him the crucial piece of information — the existence of an airport — and so we got into a taxi, leaving Charlton Jenks behind, and headed for the airport.

In the early evening we managed to get a flight, and for thirty dollars we flew to Roatán. As the plane soared over the Caribbean, we felt peaceful and relaxed, as if the worst part of our journey were done. When we got to the island, we checked into a place in downtown Roatán, a rather unappealing town. Andrew and Becky wanted to stay in town,

[205]

but Walter Weinstein in Panajachel had given me a tip on a place to stay called Roberts' Hill. Walter had said it was a peaceful, small guest house on an isolated tip of the island, run by two island people, Ruby and Robert Roberts, and I wanted to get there as soon as I could.

The town of Roatán is built on stilts for hurricanes and mud. We trudged through and checked into the Corral, a dump near a spot of sea that smelled like a sewer. The Corral had no bath or running water. I got a room near the toilet which stank all night long. Andrew and Becky took a room near mine, also adjacent to the toilets. But for the night it would do.

The Corral was three floors high with a wrap-around porch in rather shabby condition on each floor. Our rooms were off to the side, but three men and a woman sat on the porch out front. The men wore army fatigues, drank beer, and piled the bottles into a kind of fortress. They were completely soused and falling out of their chairs while the woman pranced back and forth.

We sat down on the porch near them. "So," one of the men said to me, "where you from?"

When I said we were North Americans, they all smiled. They said they were Somocistas, Nicaraguans from Somoza's National Guard. Andrew rolled his eyes and Becky looked dismayed.

That night as we were asleep someone came in my room and suddenly turned on the light. I screamed and shot out of bed. It was the woman who had been with the Nicaraguans, and she was bumbling around in my room. "I'm lost," she muttered, "I'm lost," and she staggered out again. I got up to go to the toilet. When I stepped outside, I tripped over the body of one of the drunk Nicaraguans who had collapsed earlier that evening and had been rolling around on the porch all night. I screamed, but no one came.

In the morning on our way back from breakfast, the Nicaraguans stopped us and offered to show us their boat. It was down by the water and we walked that way. The boat was small, with an outboard. One of them pulled back a tarp and revealed a pile of guns. When we returned to the Corral, the other Nicaraguans were displaying rifles. They were very drunk and very macho as they held up their pieces. "Good U.S. rifles," one of them said. He offered to let me hold it, but I declined.

Roberts' Hill sat on a small hill, about fifty yards up from the beach, on an island paradise of white beaches, coconut palms, turquoise water. It had eight rooms. The rooms had no walls, only screened-in porches with wooden louvers to shut out the wind and the rain; otherwise we were exposed to the outside. For twelve dollars a day we got a room and three very square meals.

"Well," Andrew said when we arrived, "this was a good tip." As I had been packing my bags to head to the outskirts of the island, Andrew and Becky had come to my room. They'd been planning to stay in town but were having second thoughts. "Where did you say that place was where you're going to stay?" And so they had come along.

We got settled and at noon we sat down to a family-style lunch of fresh fish fried in coconut oil, fried potatoes, some kind of greens, warm bread, and custard for dessert. When Andrew saw the platters of food, he seemed to get nervous. "How much do you plan to eat?" he asked me.

"How much do I plan to eat?" I repeated.

"I mean, do you plan to eat a lot?"

I looked at this six-foot-four, hulking man. "Not much," I replied.

Becky was laughing. "Oh, Andrew," she said, "just tell her your problem."

Andrew explained that he had a kind of anxiety attack when he had to eat family style. He came from a family of ten children and there were always thirteen people for dinner. His mother cooked enough food for seventeen and the family was served youngest to oldest. You got seconds when you finished your firsts, which meant that the oldest had to eat the fastest to get more. To this day, Andrew said, he panics when food is served family style.

I asked Andrew what it was like growing up in a family of so many children. He said it wasn't easy. Even his father had difficulty keeping everyone straight. "Once I came back from three months in Costa Rica, and my father greeted me at the airport with 'Welcome home, Jeffrey.' But Jeffrey told me not to worry," Andrew went on. "He said that Dad had been calling him Pinky on and off." Pinky, Andrew explained, was a family dog who'd died several years before.

It wasn't until evening settled in and we sat on the porch, sipping beers and watching the ocean, that we noticed Ted. Ted had been at lunch but he was at another table, and we had managed to miss him somehow. He was one of the strangest-looking people I'd ever seen. Ted had been on the island almost two months now, and one of the first things he told us was that he'd come to Roberts' Hill to recover. It occurred to us later that he'd come to recover from a sex-change operation. The problem was that we could not determine which way the operation had gone. Ted was half man, half woman. He had a woman's voice, beardless features, a man's body type and musculature, no breasts, and what appeared to be a bulge in the crotch of his shorts.

He reminded me of Truman Capote, and he knew everything about anything. He came out on the porch during cocktail hour and, once he realized Becky was a biologist, began telling us about the snakes and ticks that inhabit the island. He described Robert's encounter with a boa, which he said was eighteen to twenty feet long, thick as a coconut palm, with a red comb in its hair. Becky looked bewildered and I could see she was trying to think through her knowledge of snakes to see if such a creature was plausible.

He said he was a medical doctor with an innate sense for the stock market. During our brief cocktail hour he managed to explain how the DC-3 is a World War II plane, to direct us to the best swimming, to tell us about barracuda biting off a man's calf. He talked about head-hunters and cannibals and altered states of consciousness. He went on with Sufi legends and talk of transformation, political intrigue, and the decline of America. In this remote and peaceful place, we would never be able to get away from him/her. No matter what hour of the day or what book sat in our laps, Ted would appear, droning on and on about whatever entered his mind. And that evening as we waited for dinner, listening to the barking of a dog, Ted said the dog had found a boa. And the boas would become mythological creatures to me, like unicorns or baobab trees.

Ted told us about a canyon he liked to swim to. As he was leaving for this spot in the morning, he asked if we wanted to swim along. Though we didn't want to go with him, he knew the way, so we agreed. Andrew noticed that Ted wore a T-shirt and Bermuda shorts to go scuba diving, instead of trunks. In the week I spent on the island, Ted never took off his T-shirt and never swam in trunks, deepening our suspicions that he'd had some kind of surgery.

We swam in shallow water over thick, waving sea grass that continued almost to the reefs. We reached the canyon which was, in fact, like a canyon, and swam through it. At the bottom of the canyon a giant sea turtle was resting, and Andrew dove down and made the turtle swim. The giant turtle, sluggish, resisted at first, but Andrew dove and dove and finally the lazy turtle stretched and tediously swam away.

After several days of eating Ruby's lunches and dinners cooked in coconut oil and swimming on the reefs, Andrew and Becky decided they had to go. They asked if I wanted to come with them. They were going to Huehuetenango, but I had planned a different route for myself and also did not feel ready to leave. I accompanied them to Sandy Bay, where the rich people vacationed. Planes came down from Miami to Roatán and the Americans stayed at resorts on Sandy Bay.

We rented a boat and took it over to the bay, because

Charlie, the driver provided by Roberts' Hill, was on a binge, and there was no telling how long he would stay that way. The driver we hired sold shells and he tried to do business with us. He had conchs and shark jaws. He held up a hammerhead with seven rows of teeth — all of which rise up when the animal is ready to kill. The man, a black Carib, said that every fish out there that you ate would eat you. "You have it for dinner. It have you for lunch." Snapper, he said, was bad. "She's go to a thousand pounds and eat a cow." But what they feared, he told us, was barracuda. "Cuda can rip you apart with one bite."

We waited for the transport to take Andrew and Becky to town, and the transport was very slow, but at last it came. While we waited, we sat under a palapa sipping Cokes. On the beach two boys were having a knife fight. Vultures sat like spectators in the trees, watching them.

"Be careful in Huehue," I told them. "You know there's trouble there."

"And you be careful where you're going," they said.

The minute they left, I wished I'd gone with them. I thought perhaps I'd made a mistake by staying. I felt sad and empty to see them leave and I wondered how I would fare on the rest of this trip.

A new couple arrived, Lawrence and Felicity. They referred to each other as soul partners and said they were bonded in a spiritual way. Ted and Lawrence and Felicity seemed to have a great deal in common and over lunch all they talked about was spiritual bonding. I missed Andrew and Becky already.

In the evening Ted sat on the porch, talking to me about civil rights. "I've been punched in the face because of the way I look," he admitted. "I know I look strange. I've been refused hotel rooms." Ted was bitter about America and he said he had no intention of going home. He told me he was on a spiritual quest and was in the process of becoming a Sufi. He said that Omar Khayyám was a Sufi, and he believed that Dag Hammarskjöld was as well. He talked on about dervishes and dreams and memory and the meanings of stories. He told me a strange tale about a man and a donkey with ginger in his anus, but I didn't get the meaning, and he told me to meditate on the story and the meaning would come to me. But I've forgotten the story, and the meaning never came.

I felt troubled and restless all night long and I couldn't sleep. I was besieged as if by ghosts. A tremendous sense of loneliness came over me and I wondered if I wouldn't always be alone. If I'd spend my entire life alone, without a true traveling companion. This thought terrified me and kept me awake. It wasn't yet dawn when I got up and went outside. I sat on the porch, watching for a redheaded woodpecker with a white feathery crown, indigenous only to the Bay Islands, which Becky used to sit and watch for, and now I sat, waiting for the sunrise and for the woodpeckers to reveal themselves to me.

I had thought to myself the whole time I had been away that there would be a moment when everything would become clear, when I would understand what I had not understood before. I had been waiting for a clear moment when I would know that I'd traded cruelty for kindness, passion for companionship, anger for love. But now I knew that it would not happen this way.

As I sat out on that porch, I understood that growth comes over time. Change happens step by step. All along things had been changing inside of me, bit by bit, in small, imperceptible ways. It had been subtle, not sudden. It had been happening over time.

Before breakfast I put on my gear and went out alone in the ocean to swim to the reef, something I knew I shouldn't do, but the water out to the reefs was only about four feet deep and there was no danger of drowning. I swam for about a quarter of a mile in the warm, clear water until I realized that I was quite far from shore. In the distance I saw the now shrunken palmettos, the tiny guest house.

As I swam back, a school of blue jacks came toward me. And behind the blue jacks was a barracuda, thick waisted, several feet long. Its well-toothed jaws opened and closed as it fed in their school. The barracuda passed me and I kept swimming. I thought of Ted's tales of cuda and what the Carib man had said. I swam steadily until I noticed that now I was surrounded by the school of blue jacks — thousands of them, all around me, little blue fish, hurrying away. Turning my head slowly, I found the barracuda, its eyes set, its mouth opening and closing at my heels.

I have been told that if an animal confronts you, often the best thing to do is surrender. You cannot outrun or outswim it. It will probably maul you, but you will live. But reason left me and my stubbornness prevailed. I ripped a gold chain from my wrist, in case the glitter was attracting the barracuda, and let the bracelet, a keepsake, float out to sea. Then I took a deep breath and I swam. I swam in fast, steady strokes, at every moment expecting the cuda to rip through the muscle of my calf or tear off my heel. I swam and swam, breathing, hoping, believing, and when I reached the shore, I pulled myself up and collapsed in the sand, breathless, safe.

THINKING THAT THERE MIGHT BE SOME MAIL OR messages for me, I entered the United States Embassy in Tegucigalpa. I walked past several armed Honduran guards, through an extensive electronic device, into a Plexiglas bullet-proof chamber, where a man, himself encased in Plexiglas, asked me for my passport.

Once I was inside, this letter awaited me, dated November, a few months before:

Dearest Mary,

We assume you are well and taking good care of yourself. We, of course, are concerned, especially when we have no idea how to contact you, but I know you have a good head on your shoulders and won't do anything foolish.

Everything is fine here, though Mother had a touch of the flu. But she's getting stronger and recuperating. No need to be concerned.

I've been busy, busy, busy. We've got a new J. C. Penney going up and a big mall in the works in Waukegan. And there's talk of more in Milwaukee and points north. We've come up with a new concept. Put it all under one roof. I know that sounds crazy, but it might work. No more snow, no more rain. You just drive into an underground parking lot and you're in one gigantic store. Anyway, we're trying the idea out on the town planners in a few states and if we get the go-ahead, we're on our way.

Here's a clipping I thought you'd like to see. It's a car that was driven by your friend Linda. As you can see, she drove it off the road and the car flipped over three times, but somehow Linda only had scratches. She was wearing her seat belt. That seems to be what saved her. Goes to show you can never be too careful. Keep that in mind, wherever you are.

As you can see, there isn't much to tell here. You are leading the exciting life. For us, it's business as usual. We think of you constantly and miss you. I won't say we don't worry, but we know you'll be all right.

Mother keeps a map of Central America on the wall. Whenever we get a card or letter from you, she makes a red check. In this way, we are charting your course. Most of the time we have no idea where you are, but we try to figure it out, given the direction of where your cards are from.

We hope you will decide to come home soon. I am sending copies of this letter to our embassies in Guatemala, Belize, Honduras, Costa Rica, and Panama, but not to Salvador or Nicaragua, because I know you won't go there. Mother joins me in sending all our love.

Dad.

NICARAGUA HAS MORE ACTIVE VOLCANOES PER square mile than any other country in the world. When I arrived, they were all smoldering. It is the feeling one gets in Nicaragua. A sense of everything bubbling, boiling beneath the surface. It seemed like the fitting metaphor for this country that had just been victorious over its dictator. I had wanted to go to Nicaragua since the Sandinistas had come into power, and when the opportunity presented itself, I went.

I joined a small group of people interested in culture and we were to stay at a cultural center in Managua called the Hotelito, the little hotel. Though I was unaccustomed to this type of group travel, it was the only way for me to see Nicaragua at the time. We were assigned a guide, a petite blond woman named Tamar. Tamar came from Uruguay, where she had been imprisoned and tortured. She never discussed the details of her torture or imprisonment. She had left her own country when she was freed and had come here to work for the revolution. And that was all she'd tell us.

We drove in a bus through downtown Managua, which consisted of buildings separated by open fields. "Where is the center of the town?" I asked. Tamar looked at me and smiled. "It is everywhere," she said. "Since the earthquake we have not been able to rebuild. That is Somoza's fault. Do you know what he did? He took the blood that was sent by the Red Cross and he sold it. He put the money into his Swiss bank account. That was when the people really began to hate him. When he sold the blood."

Each day Tamar had an outing planned. The markets, a farm, co-op, a fish farm. We visited cooperative stores that sold

[215]

folkloric art and government agencies in charge of such things as elections and civil defense.

We journeyed into the Fifth Region, an area where there were said to be two thousand contras and much military activity. We were taken to a hospital, where I visited the maternity ward. A woman showed me her baby, only two hours old. In another ward a boy of about eighteen, whose stomach had been blown away in a contra attack, pulled back the covers and showed me his wound. "I am not a soldier," he said. "I work on a farm."

On the bus back to Managua I sat beside Tamar. "Are you happy here?"

"I have never been happier," she replied.

"What makes you so happy?"

She looked at me as if I were insane. "We are working for something. Our lives have meaning."

At dusk I walked through the neighborhood near the hotel. It was a poor neighborhood — houses with no water or electricity, dirt floors. Children followed me. I carried pens and pencils, key chains and candy, to give as gifts. I handed them pencils and pens. One little boy reached up and gave me a kiss. Then he ran away into his house. He came out again with a small Sandinista flag. He gave this to me as a gift. I gave him some American coins. Again he ran into his house, though I called for him to come back. He returned with a small kerchief. I said, "I will only give you something more if you promise not to go get me something else." He agreed. I gave him an Empire State Building key chain. He ran home again, though I shouted once more.

This time he returned with his mother. Is he giving his mother away, I wondered. Instead, she gestured toward her house. "Please be my guest. Come into our home." They each took me by the arm, leading me inside. The house was modest but comfortable. One room was a living room, kitchen, and den. The other was a bedroom, where it seemed that four people slept. "My husband," the woman began, "died fighting in the revolution. The government gave me this house. We are very happy here."

[216]

"And the government? You are happy with them?"

"It is a government like all others." She threw her head back, laughing. I had thought she was an old woman, but now that I saw her laughter I realized she could not be much older than I. "What can I say? And my husband died, so it is difficult. But we have more now than we ever had before."

"So you are happy with the government."

"I am happy with our revolution," she said firmly. "But these are difficult times." She extended her arms. Her children flocked around her, grabbing at her skirts, and she held them to her, as if for dear life.

A few nights later we attended an FSLN (Sandinista National Liberation Front) rally, where a quarter of a million people were shouting, *"No pasarán"* (they will not enter), and *"Un ejército"* (we are all one army). We are one people's army.

Tamar kept inching her way to the front, dragging me by the hand, until we were almost at the grandstand, and in front of me were the members of the junta. Daniel Ortega was speaking about freedom. He spoke of the elections that the Nicaraguans planned to have. He said, "A vote means to vote for the heavens, the land, the people, the flowers, the stars, the sun."

I turned to Tamar and heard her say, "Arturo, it is so good to see you again."

She embraced a man of about forty-five. He had a head of salt and pepper curls and piercing steel-gray eyes. "Tamar, I have not seen you in so long."

"Well," Tamar said, "we have been busy in cultural affairs."

"And I have been busy with the military," he said with a laugh. Tamar introduced me to a *subcomandante* of the revolution.

"He is one of our great heroes," she said softly, and I understood from her tone of voice that at some point she had cared for him and something had happened.

But Arturo blushed and shook his head. "I didn't do anything you didn't do, Tamar."

Tamar shook her head, acknowledging that neither would win this discussion. He took us each by the arm. "Come," he said. "Let's go somewhere where we can talk." And we made our way through the crowd of a quarter of a million people back toward a small stand where you could purchase beer. He bought us each a beer and we sat down.

"So," Tamar said, "where have you been keeping yourself?" She laughed, tossing her blond curls.

"Oh, I am defending borders. I am doing security checks. All day and all night long I am working. It is difficult," he said with a laugh, "this victory."

The next day on our way to a market Tamar told me about Arturo. She said he had been a journalist but had joined the underground. He had been captured and tortured for a long time. His hatred ran deep. Arturo was a victim of history, she said.

We reached the market. It was filled with flowers, coffee beans, cotton, children. We went to meet a group of women who talked about their cooperative and how it worked. On the wall were pictures of children. I asked one of the women who they were. The women grew silent until their spokeswoman said, "These are our children. They died in fighting. They are heroes of the revolution. All mothers," she said, "mourn the loss of all children. Do you have children?" she asked me. I said I did not. "When you have a child, you will know what it is to pin your child's picture to the wall."

The subcomandante came to the hotel that evening and asked if Tamar and I would like to go to a café. He drove us through the streets of Managua to a small park. Inside the park was a place to sit and have a beer. Two other women from our group had come with us and we sat at a table, talking. One of the women asked what Nicaragua would do if the United States decided to invade. Arturo laughed. "We are already preparing ourselves for the worst," he said. His steel-gray eyes sparkled as he spoke. "But try to imagine the occupation of Nicaragua. We are a people with a great capacity for covert war. We have malnutrition, but we also have tremendous experience in clandestine war. We got rid of Somoza with sticks and stones. No one is thinking about big weapons here. My biggest weapon will be I'll cut off my curls and dye my hair." He pointed to his head of curls. "I'll dye it black and shave my mustache. And I will become a citizen. An ordinary citizen, and I will kill whomever I need to kill in order to stay free. What we say here is 'free homeland or death.' Those are not just words. Nicaraguans mean this. We have a very precise, clear meaning of death. We never lose our happiness. Every day people die, but we don't lose our happiness. We are free in our hearts. They can do anything they want to my body. But they'll never touch my soul."

I don't know for how many hours Arturo continued talking in this vein, but it was a long time, and no one interrupted him. Later he drove us home. We drove through a residential neighborhood that soon turned into deserted streets, bombed-out buildings, an area resembling the South Bronx. There were no streetlights and I began to feel nervous. "Are we lost?" I asked. I looked all around me and saw nothing. "No, no," he said. "You are not lost. Don't be afraid," Arturo said. He pulled a revolver out of his hip pocket. "You are with me."

The next day we traveled to Masaya. We walked through this city of political slogans and bullet-ridden walls. It was in Masaya just a few years before that the first spontaneous insurrection against the Guardia occurred. Camillo Ortega, brother of Daniel and Humberto, died here, fighting. As we walked through Masaya, children followed. A boy of about seventeen came up to me. He said, "Are you North Americans?" I said we were. He said, "Why are you fighting with Nicaragua?"

"I don't know," I replied.

"I don't either," he said. "But I don't want to fight." He

asked me to write to him. Carefully he wrote down his name and address on a card. I gave him mine. "Please," he said, "write me a letter. I want to hear from you." He looked at me with longing eyes. "I don't want to fight," he told me. He had warm, brown eyes and he seemed very sad. "I don't want to be in a war. I am afraid I'll be killed." Now he whispered, his face pressed close to my face. "I will write to you," he said. "Then you will write back to me." I promised I would. His eyes followed me as I headed down the street.

He would write me one letter, which I answered. Then I never heard from him again.

That afternoon Arturo left a message at the cultural center, saying he would like to take Tamar and me to dinner, but at dinnertime he phoned. He had an emergency to attend to, but he said that the following evening he would pick us up at seven. The next evening, just before his car arrived, Tamar came to my room. "I'm not going with you," she said. "I have to go with a group somewhere."

"Tamar," I said, "please, I don't want to go alone."

"You'll be fine," she said. "He is a great man."

A military car came for me at seven and the driver sent Arturo's apologies. He had had to work late and would meet me at his house. I sat in the back of the limousine, equipped with walkie-talkie and, lying beside the driver's seat, an automatic rifle. I watched the landscape pass as we drove to the outskirts of Managua.

The suburbs were bucolic. Lawns, tree-lined streets, crickets chirping. It was a night that reminded me of home, of my childhood in the Midwest. I could have been driving through northern Illinois just then. I could have been anywhere. Kansas. I enjoyed the feeling of the evening. The breeze, the cooler air. At that moment, it seemed difficult to believe all that had happened here.

As we drove, the neighborhood changed. The houses grew larger, more luxurious. Later I learned that these houses had been owned by the staunch supporters of Somoza and were now lived in by high government officials. At last we pulled up in front of a house. It had a low cement wall around it and the top of the wall was covered with barbed wire. At the only entrance sat a man with a machine gun.

The driver honked and out of the dark entrance the subcomandante emerged, backlit in a halo of mist and smoke. He kissed me hello on both cheeks and led me into his house. It was a big house with a patio entrance and another patio off to the side. We entered a large living room, devoid of furnishings except for a small cot with a blanket and throw pillows, a quadraphonic sound system that blasted "Bridge Over Troubled Water," and an 11" x 14" photo of the subcomandante with Fidel Castro.

I wandered through the bleak setting. There were three bedrooms, with their doors open, and in each was only an unmade army cot for furniture. In the dining room the table was not set, and the chairs were missing. There was no sense of dinner, of cooking. No sense of a woman's presence. No sense of any personal life at all.

The music switched from Simon and Garfunkel to a tape of light rock, Muzak style, of the Beatles, then the Bee Gees and *Saturday Night Fever*, and on to the Best of Motown. Arturo led me to the side patio, where he had set up a bar and a few small dishes of nuts and cheese. I looked around, feeling awkward and surprised and not knowing what to say. So I said that his house didn't seem all that protected. "It looks as if anyone could get in," I said.

"Oh, yes, you are right. Anyone could. They just couldn't get out." He offered me a drink. I said I'd have vodka. He showed me a bottle of the best Russian vodka and poured me a drink. He talked as he poured, but the music was so loud, with four speakers blasting into the patio, that I could not hear him at all. After a while, I said, "Excuse me, Arturo, do you think we could turn the music down? I'd like to talk, but I can't hear you."

But he was obsessed with the loud music that roared through his house as if it were a disco. He changed the tape to salsa, soft jazz, and then classical — Aranjuez and the Albinoni concerto for strings — and finally Burt Bacharach, "Raindrops Keep Fallin' on My Head." He waltzed with me into a corner, away from his guards. I waltzed him back onto the patio. He kept trying to get out of the sight of his guards and I kept trying to waltz back into their view. Finally I grew tired of this dance. "Let's sit down," I said. "I want to rest."

He began to talk of his travels. He had been to India and China, to Russia and Madagascar. He had been to Tahiti and several times to New York. "Here," he said. "Here is a wonderful liquor from China." He reached across to his bar and held up a bottle. Inside the bottle was a small, coiled, dead snake. He opened up the bottle. "You must smell it," he said.

"No, thank you." I turned away.

"But you must." He held the bottle to my nose. "They drop the snake in alive," he went on, still putting the bottle to my nose. "It is an odor emitted by the dying snake," he said, "that gives the liquor its perfume."

He put the bottle away and, pouring me another drink, continued. "But the best food I have ever eaten is in North Vietnam. You know, once I ate a meal that represented the four seasons. It was a beautiful plate with white food for winter and greens for springtime and orange for autumn and yellow for summer. Another time I ate a meal that was the great rivers of the world. Each meal is symbolic. Each food, specially prepared, has some greater meaning." He handed me perhaps my fourth vodka tonic of the evening. I wasn't really counting any longer.

"But the most incredible dish I ever had," he went on, "was this delicacy from Vietnam. It is the cooking they do with monkeys. They have a soup they make with the hands and feet of monkeys — they look like a baby's hands and feet — and it is delicious to suck on these, but the most remarkable dish I ever had was monkey's brains." He leaned close to me as he spoke. "They have a special table with holes in it and in a cage they have live monkeys. They grab a monkey and stick its head through the table so that the top sticks out, and with a special knife for this purpose they slice off the top of the head. You cannot believe the screeching sound the monkey makes when this happens. Then they put a sauce on this slice of monkey head, and you eat it, just like that, raw. I have tasted many things in my life, but nothing has impressed me the way this has."

He asked if I wanted to dance again. I said I didn't. I wanted to go to the bathroom. But he took me by the arms and began waltzing. "Arturo," I said, "you are a handsome man. You are forty-five years old. Don't you have a wife somewhere? Don't you have a family?"

He waved his hand in my face. "Others do, but, well, I do and I don't." He looked away. "I gave up everything for my country." He sighed and looked down. "Everything," he said.

He reached across and tried to kiss me, and I pulled away. "I am not feeling well. I'd like to get back home."

But he didn't seem to hear. Instead, he spun across the patio, around and around, clutching me in his arms. I grew more and more dizzy until I almost collapsed. I pushed him away. "Please," I said, "I am very tired now. I have hardly eaten all day. I need to use the bathroom."

His guard showed me the way to the bathroom, and when I was finished, I looked at my watch. It was way past midnight, and still there was no sign of food. I wandered into the kitchen, thinking I'd see something that resembled dinner.

The kitchen was large and barren. It had once been white but was now a filthy gray. The floor was sticky and it took me a moment to understand that what was running everywhere was roaches. The only food I saw was a piece of bread on a small plate with roaches swarming all around it.

I thought I was going to be sick. I had no idea what to do, so I staggered back onto the patio. "I am hungry," I said, "and there is no food."

"Of course there is food," he said, angrily now. "There is

[223]

plenty of food. It is all prepared. I will go get you your food." He stomped off and returned with a plate filled with glop that looked like army food — some kind of polenta with fried pork. Then he launched into a harangue against me. He said, "You are an intellectual but you have been alienated from your intellect. You think you understand, but you have no real feeling for what we are all about." He went into a fairly poetic and elevated speech about my lack of revolutionary development. He was so furious that at last he got up and turned off the music, and all I could think was, thank God. Suddenly, for the first time that evening, it was quiet. It was unbelievably quiet. "I have no idea what your problem is," he said. "I am only trying to be hospitable. I am trying to make you understand the revolution in Nicaragua."

"I am trying to understand." I was in tears. "I think I do understand." Now, from hunger and fatigue, from drinking and fear, from anger toward him and frustration with my own limitations, I was sobbing.

He was quiet for a moment. Then he stood up and took me by the hand. "Come," he said, growing gentler. "You must see the orchard. This is where I work. This is where I get my sense of peace." He led me outside into a very pleasant orchard with peach trees and plum and mango. "Every morning at five A.M. I come here."

"It is beautiful," I said. "It is very peaceful." It really was.

"People think it is easy to keep up an orchard like this in the tropics, but it is not easy. It will not grow by itself. The sun burns it. Parasites devour it. It needs care and tending. It is like the revolution. Everything takes work and time."

"Arturo," I said, exhausted, "I must go back now."

"Won't you have a brandy?"

It was now after three in the morning. "It is almost time for you to be in your orchard," I said. "And I'll be sick if I have a brandy."

Annoyed with me once again, he snapped his fingers and

summoned his driver. After walking me to the car, he kissed me on both cheeks. As I drove away, I saw him, again backlit in that halo of mist, the armed guard behind him. When the car turned off the street, the subcomandante was still standing there, a lonely hero, his orchard of ripe fruit shimmering behind him.

10

FLIGHT

IN DREAMS I AM AN ANIMAL. I HAVE THE FUR OF A white tiger. The flight of an owl. The body of a blue whale. I dwell in jungles; my cubs are hidden in a lair in a mountainside, covered with brush. When I hunt it is from the sky. I am a night stalker — my prey only the smallest things. Lizards, mice, orange salamanders. But water is my element and it is where I love to be. I rise and breach, fall and dive. I dwell in all these places and in all places I am content to be. In dreams I am an animal. In these dreams I am free.

I know the road that lies before me. I know it well. I have traveled it before. Ten, twenty, a hundred times. In this lifetime and in others. Each turn and twist is known to me. Markers are familiar. A cactus, a donkey, a wildflower patch. I have been gone for weeks. For months, for decades, or more, but it is all there as I left it. The house, the children, Lupe. No one here will ever change or grow old. Now I am going back, and as the bus approaches, a weight lifts. My ghosts recede. I know they will all be there waiting, even if I am frail and old.

As I drag my bags up the street, the children converge, shouting, calling my name. They grab at me like hungry dogs, cling to my ankles and arms. My pockets, laden with candy, trinkets, tiny flags, are soon emptied. The children engulf me, pulling me down. I fall to my knees on the dusty road. Pollo, Lisa, Agustín, come running. More children fling themselves upon me. I am drowning in a sea of children, tossing in waves of children. Reaching out my arms, I let them take me to the ground, into the dust, and they climb all over me, laughing.

I could not remember what my body looked like. It had been months since I had last seen it in a full-length mirror. I tried to catch a glimpse of my shape in windows as I passed, but the glass is old in San Miguel, and what came to me was a distortion.

One day when Lupe and María Elena were bathing Pollo in my kitchen sink, I asked them, "Have I gotten fat?"

They both looked at me, amazed by the question. Lupe took it very seriously. "No, but you are *gordita*."

"Gordita?" This means chubby. I was enraged. "How can you say I am gordita?" I ran my hands over my body, which felt firm to me, strong. Suddenly I was an Amazon, ready to do battle. Lupe squeezed my arm to me. She tugged at a ripple of flesh. "Gordita," she confirmed.

María Elena nodded. "It is not unattractive," she said. María Elena, though pregnant, remained bone thin. She pinched her own arm. "It is better than this chicken's leg."

I poked at Lupe's belly and she jumped away. "I am having a baby," she said.

"Not here." I laughed, jabbing her in the sides, grabbing handfuls of flesh as she tried to run away.

"You are old and gordita," Lupe taunted me as I chased her through the room.

At night I lay in bed, running my hands across my thighs, my belly, my breasts. I was blind to myself. I could not see what others saw; I had no sense of how others saw me. I was disappearing in space. Time also slipped away. I lost track of the days. Every day was Sunday.

THOUGH IT WAS TOO EARLY FOR THE RAINY SEASON, it rained every day. The electricity failed and I could not work. My typewriter lay idle. I returned to pen and paper, but I needed something to drown out the noise of the construction next door. It began early every morning, and sometimes I would go to my roof and look down. It seemed they were building an enormous enclosed chicken farm next door to me. I did not like the man who owned the house. Often at five in the morning he started his trucks, and the exhaust went right into my bedroom. One morning I woke, almost suffocating with carbon monoxide poisoning. I went to the roof and shouted at him. "Can't you point your truck the other way?"

He shouted back. "I am loading chickens. I cannot load them from the front."

In the afternoon I'd walk the hills, thinking I should really find something productive to do, but I'd pick wildflowers instead, and talk to the sky.

One day I returned from market and found Lupe waiting for me, distraught. "Oh, María," she called, "the federales were here, looking for you. Have you done something wrong?"

"What did they say?" I was sure they had made a mistake.

"They said they would be back."

A few days later, a carload of federales pulled up in front of my apartment. They could have been sent by central casting. They were fat and carried enormous guns. The chief had a handlebar mustache, which he twirled ominously as he spoke. "Doctor," he called me for some reason, "your visa has expired. You must leave the country."

"But sir," I said obsequiously, "I am involved in important

work and cannot leave at this time. Can't you grant me an extension?"

"We have been sent by immigration, Doctor. You must return to your own country. At the border you will be issued a new visa."

For a moment I thought they would deport me then and there, but they gave me two weeks. "If you are not gone by then, Doctor, well, we will have to come for you again."

Though I had seen Alejandro only sporadically in the past few weeks, he had written to say he'd visit on the weekend. When he arrived in Carlos's car, which he'd borrowed, I told him about the visit from the federales.

"Oh, it's a technicality. It's a bureaucratic matter," he said.

"I know, but it seems I can't renew it on this end."

"Oh, these federales . . . Didn't you bribe them?"

I shrugged. "It never occurred to me."

"Well, you'll have to come to Mexico City and we'll clear this matter up."

I didn't want to go to Mexico City. In fact, I couldn't bear the thought. "Come and stay with me for a while," Alejandro said.

"I don't know if it's a good idea."

"Well, I have a surprise for you. I have moved to a new apartment. It is much bigger, with three bedrooms, and you will have your own room to work in."

I was fearful of not having a renewed visa when the federales returned, and so somewhat reluctantly and against my better judgment, I went to Mexico City to try to straighten out my immigration problems and to live with Alejandro for a while.

I believe in miracles. I always have. I believe that incredible things can happen if we recognize the signs, if we know how to watch for them. Things happen to us for reasons, and we must accept our fate, even if it makes no sense to us at the time. I believe it was my fate, thanks to the federales, that led me back to Mexico City. I believe that a part of me knew what was going to happen and that I went there in order to survive.

We packed up the few things I needed and set out at the end of the weekend. We drove down the road with the dangerous curves, down the dusty road toward the main highway to Mexico City. We were happy, laughing, and we stopped to buy oranges. Then we reached Avenida de Torres, Number Eight, where I was to live for a while.

The apartment was in a gigantic housing project almost an hour outside the center of town. The project must have consisted of ten thousand units, all of them the same. The grounds around the project had not been completed, and so the whole neighborhood was a swirl of dust and construction debris. The apartment was on the ground floor and consisted of cement walls and a cement floor. The windows had bars on them and it was, for all purposes, the equivalent of a cell block.

I didn't know what to do or say. "I can't live here," I blurted out. "I can't stay." I sat down on the bed, weeping. He had moved in part on my account, and though I had told him not to do this, he had done it, and I felt responsible. I also felt trapped. I knew somehow I had to stay.

My time in that dust-ridden barren tenement dwelling was like solitary confinement to me. We still had no phone, no way of communicating with anyone. When Alejandro left for work at seven I was completely alone, isolated for hours in a place where I hated to be. Sometimes I'd go to the pay phone outside and make frantic calls to the States. Women from the project, their hair in curlers, would line up impatiently behind me. They smoked cigarettes while screaming children, like monkeys on leashes, dangled from them.

Other afternoons I'd visit the embassy or the immigration office and try to find someone who would give me a new visa without much grief. I went from bureaucrat to bureaucrat, doing everything I could except what I knew would get me a new visa — grease a palm. One gave me a two-week extension. Another told me to forget about it. A third threatened me with jail, and I lied to him about my address, petrified that he'd track me down and I'd go to jail for lying to the immigration service. (The resolution would only come when I crossed into Guatemala on another trip. My old visa was taken from me by a distracted border guard whom I captured with a smile and a glance. He did not notice that it was long expired, and a new one was issued upon my return, ending months of turmoil and irrational fear.)

I buried myself in work, and when I could do that no longer, I went into the center of Mexico City. I worked at a library or a museum and left Alejandro messages telling him where to meet me. There were other diversions. The arrival of Marta in a frantic, melodramatic state. An earthquake that rocked me from my stupor. A letter that was slipped under the door weeks after it was sent. But mostly I lived a pale life without excitement. I don't know why I stayed, but I stayed and stayed even though I longed to be in San Miguel.

One evening in the spring Alejandro and I went to a movie, and in the middle of the film, I felt a pain in my side. As the movie continued, the pain worsened, and finally I told Alejandro, "Something is the matter with me."

I could not straighten up as we walked from the theater. I stumbled out, bent over. He helped me until we got to a pharmacy. The pharmacist said I must have amoebas, and he gave me some medicine. We took a taxi home. The pain was terrible until I got into bed and lay perfectly still. If I didn't move, there was no pain. I told this to Alejandro. "It only hurts when I laugh." Then I recalled that this was what the cowboys often said in the old Westerns, just before they died.

The next day I stayed in bed, moving in and out of sleep, thinking that I'd feel better soon and that it was just a stomachache. But then the pain came back, worse than before, and at times I felt as if my side would split in two, like a melon. I dozed in and out and then I woke in the middle of the night. My body was drenched; the bed around me was soaking wet, as if someone had tossed a bucket of water on me. The pain in my side radiated through my body.

I woke Alejandro. "You must get me to the hospital."

He looked at me, annoyed, and shook his head. "I can't get a cab now. You have to wait until morning."

"You must get a cab and get me to the hospital now."

He threw off his covers. "I'll never find a cab."

"You have to," I said.

I managed to dress and toss some things into a bag while he went outside. Then I lay there, breathing deeply, praying that the time would pass quickly, but it did not. It was slow and long, but finally Alejandro came running inside.

The cab sped through Mexico City in the predawn light. It would take about forty-five minutes to reach the hospital. At each bump and each stop, I clutched myself with pain. On the Paseo de la Reforma we came to a stoplight, and a boy of about fifteen appeared in the intersection, blocking our cab. He had a torch which he ignited and proceeded to swallow. This late-night fire-eater, perhaps returning home, stood in front of us, spitting fire into the blue-green sky. "Give him something," I told Alejandro. He gave the boy five pesos and we drove away.

When we reached the hospital, I could hardly move. For hours, it seemed, I lay on a table as doctors probed and examined and nurses came and went. White was everywhere. One nurse came in the most frequently. She had a chart and every ten minutes or so took my temperature, my pulse, and my blood pressure, checking my vital signs. Finally I grew weary of the examinations. "Why are you doing this?" I asked.

"Just keeping tabs on you," she said.

"What's my temperature?"

She hesitated, but then told me it was a hundred and five. "And my pressure."

She read from her chart. Sixty/forty. And finally she told

me that my pulse was one hundred thirty. I remember thinking to myself as I drifted off to sleep that once I'd run the six miles around Central Park and when I'd finished that run, my pulse was one hundred thirty.

"I'm dying," I said.

She looked at me oddly, then walked away.

I did not know what time it was when the door opened and a tall, dark man whom I recognized immediately walked in. He was the man in my dream of the wounded cat, the one who had washed her insides. He paused and looked at me for a long time. "I know you," he said.

"I'm the woman who brought in those two Chicano women, the ones in the car accident six months ago."

Dr. Cruz nodded. He wrapped his fingers tightly around my arm. "I won't let anything happen to you," he said.

It was Dr. Cruz who discovered what was wrong with me. "You have some kind of an infection that has ruptured. An abscess of some sort. We call it peritonitis."

"What are you going to do?"

He looked at me hard. "I have to operate. You are lucky to be here. If you'd been in San Miguel, you wouldn't have made it."

I must have looked frightened because he squeezed my arm again. "You'll be all right," he said.

"I know."

He smiled. "How do you know?"

"I dreamed it," I said.

WHEN I WAS WELL ENOUGH TO TRAVEL, I WENT TO San Miguel to recuperate. Alejandro thought I was crazy, but I wanted to go. "Nothing worse can happen to me," I reasoned. "Please take me. I want to go." He borrowed a car, took some time off from school, and drove me to San Miguel. I slept the entire way. When we reached my house, I could barely walk upstairs.

I was in bed much of the day with Lupe and the children bringing me fresh flowers and newborn animals. María Elena sat downstairs, ripe now and moping, abandoned by her lover, mashing beans or washing lettuce. She looked like a giant beetle with her enormous belly and skinny arms and limbs.

Alejandro was involved in the endless preparation of elaborate Mexican dishes which I could hardly bring myself to eat. He would bring them up on trays and would sit watching until I finished every bite. He hovered over me, insisting I stay in bed and asking at each moment what he could do. After a while it occurred to me that somehow he was enjoying the fact that I was ill and couldn't take care of myself. One day he brought me a tray, and I said, "Don't pamper me. I'll get out of bed." And stubbornly, painfully, I did this. I grew irritable with him until I said to him, "I'm not good for you. I'm not making you happy."

"But I love you," he protested.

"For all the wrong reasons," I replied.

Then he got very angry. "You used me. Just like all your gringos. You think you can come down here and use me."

I was too ill to argue with him. "It has nothing to do with that. We're just not right for each other, that's all."

He stayed around for a few more days, growing silent and

remote. Finally I asked him to leave. "I want you to go back to Mexico City," I said. In the afternoon he left, and I felt relieved. I promised him I'd see him soon, but I wasn't sure when that would be.

After he was gone, Lupe came and kneeled down at my bed. She wrapped her hands around mine and rested her face on my hands. "Will you stay?"

"For a while," I said. "Until I feel better. But then I'm going away."

"On another trip."

"Yes," I said rather wistfully, realizing that I had begun to think about going home. "On another trip."

It was then that I noticed that Globo was missing. "Lupe," I said, "where's the cat?"

Lupe looked very sad, as if somehow she was responsible. "She died. We found her dead."

"When? When did she die?"

Lupe thought for a moment. "It was on Friday. Two days after my birthday." Lupe's birthday had been a week before, and I had sent her a card. Two days after, when Globo died, was the day Dr. Cruz operated on me.

I was sleeping the next day when Derek Armstrong came by. He carried a bunch of half-dead snapdragons and a package under his arm. "My God, I heard you almost died in Mexico City. Incredible. That's what you get for screwing a spic. Here." He thrust the wilted snapdragons into my hand. "This is to cheer you up."

"Oh, thanks. Listen, I'm not feeling too well."

"That's why I came by. To do you a favor."

"A favor? That's nice."

"I thought I'd let you be the first person to read the unexpurgated first draft of *Flat on My Face*."

"What's that?"

"My novel."

"Your novel? You finished your novel?" He tore open the package and thrust several hundred pages into my hands, beaming. "I don't want to read it," I said.

He looked dumbfounded. "What?"

"I'm not strong enough." I handed it back to him. "I don't want to read it."

"Well, how about a chapter, then? It'll give you something to do."

"I don't need anything to do. Now get out." He dangled his chapter before my nose. "Get out."

That night as I lay reading in bed, the rains came. Heavy torrential rains and I knew the season was about to begin. It was not long before the lights went out. I found the matches I kept in the drawer by the bed and lit the candles on the nightstand. I took a candle downstairs to locate my Eveready flashlight. Just as I found the flashlight in the drawer, there was a knock. "María, are you all right?"

I opened the door and found Lupe with the smallest children. She had candles in her hand. "I'm fine," I told her. "You don't have to worry about me." Then I kissed the children and said good night.

I LANDED AT SANTA ELENA AIRPORT OUTSIDE Flores, prepared to begin my final jungle venture. This was the region of El Petén in Guatemala and the scene of the ruins of Tikal — the great Mayan center that had flourished, been abandoned, and, like the other great centers, been consumed by the jungle. I arrived late in Flores, an almost mystical city on an island in the middle of a steaming lake. There was a fiesta in town that night, and for a few hours I walked among the carnival rides, the lights, the clowns and popcorn.

In the morning I woke at four-thirty, dragged myself out of bed, and got the five-thirty bus to Tikal. I rode half-asleep through the tropical land. As we approached, toucans flew out of trees. Parrots squawked overhead. I was about to enter Tikal National Park, perhaps the greatest and most mysterious of the Mayan ruins.

I reached Tikal at about seven and checked into the Jungle Lodge, one of the three accommodations there, all of which were pretty bad — just a step above the straw-mat place at Jocotán on the Honduran border. The Jungle Lodge consisted mainly of a large room with partitions separating sleeping quarters but providing no privacy from sounds. The food would be indescribably bad — I have no memory of having eaten a thing for the two days — and I would spend my entire time there wishing I'd brought a bag of groceries. But the location was pleasant, right at the edge of the jungle. After dropping my duffel in my cubicle, I went out for a walk.

I headed into the thick, tropical rain forest, down paths covered with lianas. Toucans and amazing blue morphos were everywhere. As I passed one tree, a dozen or more toucans, with those incredible orange and yellow beaks, flew from it. I moved deeper into the jungle. A giant rodent the size of a small pig crossed the path in front of me. It looked like a souped-up hot rod, its hind legs raised well above its front. I learned later that in this jungle the world's largest rodent lives.

Everything seemed to come in enormous proportions — the ants, the spiders, the butterflies, the birds — and this frightened me. Soon it began to rain and I headed back. The rain would last the rest of the day and into the night.

Back at the lodge I met an American woman from San Francisco. That night by candlelight she gave me pressure-point massage, which I thought was pure witchcraft, especially when she put her hands over me in order to let the energy flow through. She told me that the blending of auras had a crystallizing effect and would remove the stress from both of us. I didn't care much for the hocus-pocus, but the massage felt good.

Then a crazy Guatemalan tour director who seemed interested in at least one of us appeared at my door. He announced that it was his birthday and he wanted us to help him celebrate, but I wasn't interested. I crawled into my damp, mildewed bed. The feeling of the sheets and straw was awful, clammy to my skin, and it took a while to settle down to sleep.

The rain was heavy all night long. When I went outside in the morning I found fish swimming in the road. They had swum out of the river and into the streams of rain. I reached down and picked up one with my hand, but it writhed and slipped away. It went on swimming up the road, away from its stream and into the jungle, where it would die. You are going the wrong way, I wanted to tell it, but I didn't know how.

That afternoon when the sun emerged, I set out. I walked back toward the main pyramids, through the center plaza of the ruins. I kept going, past the Japanese tourists trudging up and down the ruins, past the Americans with dozens of lenses around their necks. I went deeper into the jungle. I met a man who told me he'd seen an ocelot, and I went in the direction he pointed.

Leaving them all behind, I crossed the main plaza and headed deeper, to the farther reaches. For the first time in what seemed like a very long time I found myself physically alone. There were no tourists, no friends, no lover to distract me. Like a person about to die, I felt my life come rushing back to me.

It was a decade ago that I lost my way. Somewhere between the Midwest and Manhattan, childhood and old age, between college and life, I arrived at a desert more vast than the Gobi, more empty than space. My purpose escaped me; the meaning was lost. For a long time I lived in an American city in an L-shaped room that looked onto an air shaft. I used to spend hours gazing down into that shaft, until one day the woman who lived across from me stood at her window and shook her head, as if scolding me. "No," she mouthed. With her hand, she shooed me away. I had had no thoughts of jumping, but only then did I realize how I'd been gazing into the abyss.

Late at night I would get phone calls for someone named Marian. They were always obscene and it was always the same man calling. He'd tell me what he wanted to do to me and where he'd place his lips. It seemed as if he knew me, since he knew just what I'd want him to do. I listened attentively, but after a half dozen calls, I grew afraid. "I'm not Marian," I told him. "You've got the wrong number." "Oh, I'm so sorry," he said. "I'm so very sorry." There was something genuine in his voice. I never heard from him again and for a time I missed him. Some nights I lay awake, trying to picture Marian in a singles' bar, giving out my phone number on slips of paper, perhaps not realizing how I was a woman like her, alone and full of wonder.

That was what I'd left behind, but it came back to me as

I stood in the jungles of Tikal, surprised at how easy it was to be with myself. It was then, standing there, that I heard the screeches. The trees shook and water tumbled on me as if it were raining, only it was not. I looked up and saw the trees filled with monkeys — howler monkeys and spider monkeys — screeching at me, jumping from branch to branch, disappearing into the haunted ruins. Toucans flew. Macaws hovered overhead. The animals that had eluded me for so long were there, raucous, wild, mocking. They hurled fruit and laughed and performed wonderful acrobatic feats for me. I stayed and watched them until dusk, when it was time to leave.

I WENT TO THE PYRAMIDS OF TEOTIHUACÁN, IN THE middle of the great Aztec plain, and stood at the place of sacrifice, where men were flayed or decapitated, their blood drained or their hearts plucked out, depending on the god to whom they were being sacrificed. I stood here at the place where Quetzalcóatl opposed Huitzilopochtli, the god of the sun and war, at the place where the female principle warred against the male principle.

My ghosts give way to the gods. I stand alone, at the top of the Pyramid of the Sun, volcanoes on either side, the wind bearing down. I have come to sacrifice myself as the warrior knights did. To let my heart be plucked out so I can become an eagle and fly closest to the sun.

I think of the eagle of my schoolgirl days, the one in that tree not far from my Midwestern home. I wonder if he was not a warrior knight who sacrificed himself to become an eagle, a companion to the sun, so that he could accompany the sun on its journey to the heights. Women were not permitted to be sacrificed in this way. Their tasks were more mundane. The grinding of corn, the weaving of cloth. Their sacrifice was of a more worldly kind. But I want to do something different with my life.

I lay my body down on the sacrificial stone and bare my chest. The wind blows off the plain to the pyramid where I lie. My breasts are large and full. The knife slices and my ribs are pulled back. Birds fly out, leaving white plumes around me. My heart throbs, resilient, and in an instant it is plucked clean, held high. And suddenly I am rid of my body. I am the first woman to be granted this privilege, to be sacrificed to the sun, to be free of my body and free to fly.

I feel my arms grow light and feathery, my body weight

decreasing, my bones turning small and frail, and soon I feel myself flapping, reaching up. I soar across this plain that has for so long kept me from going home. I am heading north. I become the eagle of my childhood vision, the traveler eagle, great visiting bird. But now my purpose is different. From on high I watch the birth of many things — seedlings and rabbits. I see donkeys foal, humans moan in travail. I go up and down. The land recedes. I am the only female in the sky. I love my feathers, my beautiful plumes. I love my glide and my dips. My sight is excellent. I fly to the high places and I am happy to perch on high.

I fly to the land of the firebird, to the Ukrainian village where my grandmother was born, and there I see her, a young girl with the palest of eyes. She wears a pale blue dress and carts water back from the well. I see her brother as he buries a live dog in the mud — this burying alive learned from his mother, who buried her children alive when the Cossacks rode through, only the dog will not live through his ordeal, and Dave, ninety-three years later on his deathbed, will say, laughing, what a cruel thing he's done. And I see a cousin of mine, a small child, being pierced on a Cossack sword, dying a sudden and terrible death. His soul will never rest.

I perch high above the house. I drink black tea, suck sugar in my beak, and munch on dried bread, and when it is time for them to leave for America, I follow. I fly. I must go and build my nest. Return to my places on high, search out the Rockies and some jagged cliff.

A male finds me and we mate, almost in midair. He hovers over my back and our wings enfold; we float in the air. I zigzag, gathering bits of twig, sagebrush, and grass. I am an eagle woman, a builder now, layer of eggs, perched on high, a woman of both heights and heart. I lay two perfect eggs, white and round. My mate disappears, but for forty-two days I sit and wait, and then they hatch.

I care for these young until the fledglings go. And then I am free to fly to new places. I sail north and south and then

I go to a place where I know I do not belong. I fly to the Midwest. I fly to a tree in a small woods near a lake, and there I rest. I do not know for how long I rest. When I wake I see a small girl standing by the side of the road, watching me. She watches and watches, and I know what is in her eyes. She wants to come with me. She is asking for the way. As I look closely, I see who she is. I open my wings, because she is asking, and I take her in.

I NEEDED TO GO TO SAN MIGUEL TO CLOSE UP MY affairs, to rent my place, and to say good-bye. It was a journey I did not look forward to making, but I knew I must. I planned to stay in San Miguel for only a few days. Then I would leave. Lupe knew I would be going, and she was prepared for this. It was myself I had to prepare.

When I arrived, the house was clean and full of fresh flowers. I did not know how it was that Lupe knew I was coming, but somehow she did. When I knocked at her door, she let me in. She said she thought I'd be coming soon. I told her I only had a few days and then I must leave. She nodded and said, "Take me with you." I looked at the children, clinging to her skirt.

"You would be unhappy where I am going," I said, and I meant it. I wondered if I wouldn't be unhappy as well. But I couldn't think of this now. It was time for me to go back. I knew that.

Lupe looked very sad. "Where is José Luis?" I asked, peering into her rooms that seemed barren, into the backyard devoid of wood.

"He left with one of his señoras. It has been a while now."

Somehow I sensed that something else was making her sad. In the corner I saw a baby's crib and suddenly the baby started crying. "Lupe, where did you get that baby?" I looked at her stomach. She was still pregnant, but due any day.

"It is María Elena's," she said.

"Your grandchild?" I embraced her. "Congratulations. We must celebrate. Where is María Elena?"

Lupe reached down to pick up the child. "She is dead. She died giving birth." Lupe handed me the baby. "We called her María." I held the baby to me. "After you."

I spent a day or so packing up my things and subletting my apartment to a student named Ralph, who went everywhere with a mangy parrot that had plucked off most of its feathers. I arranged the sublet with the Señora and soon it was done and there was nothing left for me to do except say good-bye.

My last night in San Miguel I invited Lupe and the children for dinner. Lupe and I went to market in the afternoon and bought chicken and rice, avocados and noodles for soup, and we made a dinner for ourselves. We cooked almost in silence, and from time to time Lupe ran off to care for the infant, María, and I went on the roof to see if my laundry was dry. From the roof I saw Pollo and Lisa in their red and white school uniforms, returning home. I saw the other children of San Antonio, all in uniforms, playing in the unpaved roads. I stood on the roof and saw San Miguel and the desert I had grown to care for. It was a place I could, in a sense, call home, and I realized it had been a healing place, a place that brought me peace.

We sat down and ate while the baby slept in a basket. Lisa, Pollo, and Agustín sat on the sofa. We took plates of food to the other children. As we ate, Lupe and I barely talked, and I was aware of an awkwardness and a sadness between us. "Lupe," I said, "I will be back. We will stay friends."

She nodded. "Yes, but you are going far away."

I didn't know what to say, and in fact, I wondered if I would be back. "We will write. Your children can help you with the letters."

Again there was a silence and all I could hear was the sound of crickets, a million crickets chirping in the night. "Listen," I said. "Crickets. I love the sound of crickets."

Lupe shook her head. "I don't like them. They make me sad. They make me think of something I don't want to remember."

"What's that?"

And she told me about when she was a young orphan girl and had to tend the sheep. One day she was very tired and she fell asleep. When she woke, two lambs had been killed by a coyote. When the old farm couple whom she worked for found out, they made her go to bed without food, and she was hungry all night. "And all night long," she said, "the crickets chirped. And whenever I hear the crickets, I think of the night when I was hungry, and I never want to be hungry again." There were tears in her eyes as she said this. "I never want my children to go hungry."

I reached my hand across the table. "You won't," I told her. "And they won't. I promise you that," and I meant it.

In the morning I walked down by the lake, even though it was a long way to go, to say good-bye to this place stone by stone. I walked and walked down the dusty road that led to the little white chapel near the lake. I went into the chapel for a short time to be with myself. I thought of the promise I'd made Lupe the night before, that she wouldn't be hungry again, and I thought of how I'd keep that. She had learned now how to sign her name. I decided I'd open a bank account for Lupe so I could send money when she needed it.

Content with this decision, I returned home along the sierra by my usual path. Some children followed me for a time, then dropped back. I climbed and climbed past the wildflowers and cactuses, to the highest parts of the hills, and then walked on the trail along the perimeter.

I hadn't walked for long when I saw the old woman who lived in the cave, higher up. She came out and watched me as I had seen her do many times before. I waved, but she just stood there and watched. She wore a sackcloth, and though she had a shawl around her head, I saw her silken hair down to her waist. She was beautiful, and she was old. She seemed to be watching over someone or something, and I asked her silently to look after Lupe and her children for me.

I waved and tried to walk toward her, but as always she turned quickly. All I saw as she ran off was her long stream of black hair, which turned silver in the sunlight, and then, as she disappeared into her cave, it flashed white as snow. Perhaps it was only a trick of the light, but it did not matter. I knew who she was. I recognized her now as one of the ghosts of this place, as I was soon to be counted among its ghosts.